The **I**

...to the Y

Mark ͏

The complete and unique guide
to a circular walk in the Yorkshire Dales

(IWP)

InnWay Publications

The Inn Way...to the Yorkshire Dales
© Mark Reid 1997

First Edition March 1997
(first published by Ashridge Press)
Second Edition August 1997; reprinted November 1997
Third Edition May 1999; reprinted 2000, 2002 and 2005
Fourth Edition October 2008
Reprinted June 2010

All rights reserved, no part of this publication may be reproduced, stored in a retrieval system, or transmitted, in any form or by any means electronic, mechanical, photocopying, recording or otherwise, without permission in writing from INNWAY PUBLICATIONS.

A catalogue record for this book is available from the British Library.
British Library Cataloguing in Publication Data.

All maps within this publication are based upon Ordnance Survey mapping reproduced by permission of Ordnance Survey on behalf of The Controller of Her Majesty's Stationery Office
© Crown Copyright, Licence Number: 100011978

The contents of this publication are believed correct at time of copyright. Nevertheless the author cannot accept responsibility for errors and omissions, or for changes in details given. The information contained within this publication is intended only as a general guide.

This is a long distance walk that, in some places, crosses remote and rough terrain with rocky ground and steep sections. Navigation may be difficult across the high moors and fells in poor weather; OS maps and compass essential. Walking and outdoor activities can be strenuous and individuals must ensure that they have suitable outdoor clothing, footwear, provisions, equipment, maps and are suitably fit before starting the walk; inexperienced walkers should be supervised. You are responsible for your own safety and for others in your care, so be prepared for the unexpected - make sure you are fully equipped for the hills.

'The Inn Way' is a Registered Trademark of Mark Reid.

Published by:
INNWAY PUBLICATIONS
102 LEEDS ROAD
HARROGATE
HG2 8HB

ISBN: 978-1-902001-16-6

www.innway.co.uk

The Inn Way

...to the Yorkshire Dales

The complete and unique guide to a circular walk in the Yorkshire Dales.

✦

The Inn Way...to the Yorkshire Dales is a 76-mile (122-km) circular walk divided into six day stages. Detailed maps, route descriptions, fascinating historical quotations, snippets and pieces of information will help guide you through eleven of the most beautiful valleys in the world, passing no less than 26 traditional English pubs and leaving you with a deeper knowledge and understanding of the Yorkshire Dales.

From that life-changing moment on Bellerby Moor, to a lifetime of joyous freedom and exploration of the Yorkshire Dales.

✦

Thank you to Bernadette, Stewart and Simon Reid, Paul Stokes, Peter and Susan Hughes, Matthew Hunt, Carole Rangeley, Anne and Judy Shepherd for being my walking companions whilst researching the route for the First Edition between 1994 and 1996. Thank you to the many thousands of people who have walked the route since.

Thank you to Bernadette Reid, Chris Bates and Michael Freeman who assisted with proof reading the First Edition.

I gratefully acknowledge the permission given by the authors and publishers of the books used for the short quotations throughout this publication. Every effort has been made to trace the copyright holders for these quotations. Unfortunately in some instances I have been unable to do so and would therefore be grateful for any information that may assist me in contacting these copyright holders. Full credits to author and title have been given within the text as well as in the comprehensive bibliography at the back of this book.

Front cover photograph: 'Barns and walls, Gunnerside Bottoms, Swaledale'
© Mike Kipling www.mikekipling.com

Back cover photograph: 'Swing Bridge across the Swale'
© Giles Rocholl www.gilesrocholl.com

Back cover photograph: 'Kings Arms, Askrigg' © Mark Reid
8-page colour photographs insert © Mark Reid

Illustrations © John A. Ives, Dringhouses, York.
www.johnaives.co.uk

Printed and bound by Spectrum Print, Cleethorpes.

This guidebook was researched, written, typeset, printed and bound in England.

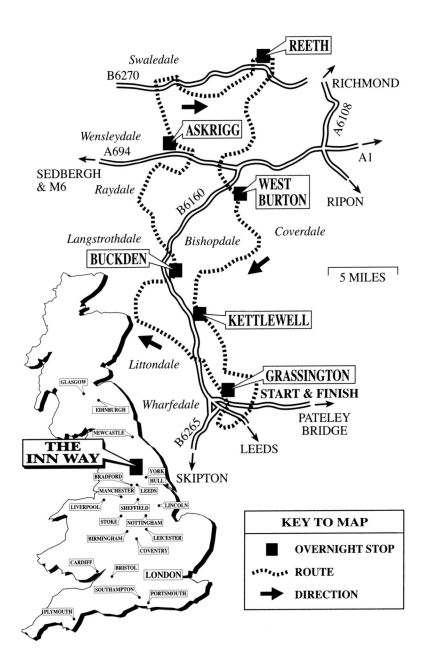

REETH

Swaledale
B6270

RICHMOND

A6108

Wensleydale
A694

ASKRIGG

A1

SEDBERGH
& M6

Raydale

RIPON

B6160

WEST
BURTON

Coverdale

Langstrothdale

Bishopdale

BUCKDEN

5 MILES

KETTLEWELL

Littondale

GRASSINGTON
START & FINISH

PATELEY
BRIDGE

GLASGOW

EDINBURGH

Wharfedale

NEWCASTLE

B6265

LEEDS

THE
INN WAY

YORK
HULL
LEEDS

SKIPTON

BRADFORD
MANCHESTER

LIVERPOOL

SHEFFIELD

LINCOLN

STOKE

NOTTINGHAM

BIRMINGHAM

LEICESTER

COVENTRY

CARDIFF

BRISTOL

LONDON

SOUTHAMPTON

PORTSMOUTH

PLYMOUTH

KEY TO MAP	
■	OVERNIGHT STOP
▪▪▪▪▪▪	ROUTE
➤	DIRECTION

A FOREWORD BY LUKE CASEY

Writer and presenter of Yorkshire/Tyne-Tees Television's
'The Dales Diary'.

I have read this latest edition of Mark Reid's excellent book with admiration and gratitude. Admiration for the way he has so thoughtfully combined fascinating fact with a superb guide which, by including twenty six thirst-slaking country inns, treats walkers as human beings rather than automatons in boots. And gratitude because now I have a volume I can lend to energetic friends without the fear that they'll be disappointed.

People who have never done it before but would love to have a go often ask me to suggest a nice Dales walk. After years of exploring the hidden treasures of this unique and beautiful part of the world, such a request, you would imagine, ought not to pose too much of a problem for me. But it always does. The reason is that when you send someone on their very first venture into your beloved hill country you want it to be a special experience for them. If only you could wave a magic wand and make the route you recommend yield up a lifetime of delights all in one go. Dales trekkers who share this love of the place will recognise the special moments:

Walking across a heather moor with a haze of pollen rising above an undulating sea of purple;

Watching the constantly shifting light unveil swathe after swathe of brilliant green on distant hills;

Listening to the chorus of hidden wild things telling their world that all is well;

Feeling, in that exquisite moment, part of it all and close to something greater than the squalid world of greed and inhumanity.

Of course, in my heart of hearts, I know there really is no need for magic wands. If music has charms to soothe the savage breast, the Dales have charms to seduce the sympathetic traveller. Time after time, confounding my fears, friends return from a recommended walk exuding contentment and peace. There is no need to ask if the hills have spoken to them. I can see it in their eyes.

Cheers to Mark Reid and The Inn Way for bringing a smile to mine.

CONTENTS

THE INN WAY

There is only one way to really experience the Yorkshire Dales and that is to pull on your boots and spend several days walking through it. A walk is all about the journey, not the destination, and travelling slowly on foot will allow more time to savour the special qualities that make the Dales so unique - the landscape, wildlife, weather, architecture, culture, people and pubs. Something always happens along the way, something that will stay as a precious memory in years to come... a farmer working his sheepdog on a hillside, the 'cackle' of a red grouse as it takes flight high on the heather moors, the vivid colour of a hay-meadow in June, a sharp bracing shower on the high fells or the smell of a coal fire drifting in the air on a cool autumnal afternoon. The hills and dales have a soothing yet inspiring quality that provides the perfect backdrop to help clear your mind and revitalise your spirit. Six days spent walking through the heart of the Yorkshire Dales will give you a fresh perspective on life and memories that will remain with you forever.

Perhaps the best part of a long walk across the hills is the 'home coming'. With fading light, you drop down along an old stony track worn by centuries of use towards the cluster of houses with twinkling lights and rising smoke. You lift the door-latch of the village pub and are enveloped by the warmth of a Dales' inn with a glowing fire in the grate and a friendly smile behind the bar. You have earned this food and drink. The traditional Dales pub with its stone-flagged floor, low beams, open fire and local ales is as much a part of the Yorkshire Dales as the fells and valleys. For me, what sets a great country pub apart is that once sat down with your pint you want to stay there all night; contentedly tired and relaxed, chatting about the day's adventures, resting weary legs, recharging your batteries. This is something to be experienced - in fact, writing about it makes me want to get out there amongst the hills, woods, streams and meadows of the Yorkshire Dales and live it, carefully planned of course to finish at a good pub!

Mark Reid, June 2005

INTRODUCTION

I grew up in the spa town of Harrogate, which is situated on the lower eastern flanks of the Pennines, and I have many fond childhood memories of the Yorkshire Dales; nervously walking behind Hardraw Force whilst clinging to the rock face, paddling in the River Ure at Aysgarth and scrambling amongst the rocks at Brimham. But I can clearly remember the moment when I fell in love with the Dales. It was a warm Saturday afternoon in May 1985 and my parents drove me from Harrogate to Reeth to perform in my school band as part of the Swaledale Festival that evening. The other band members had travelled earlier in the day but unfortunately I had to revise for my fast approaching 'O' Levels. It was as we crossed Bellerby Moor and started to drop down towards Swaledale that my mother pulled the car off the unfenced road to admire the view. I got out of the car and stood there completely captivated by what I saw; the heather clad moorland swept down to the valley of the Swale, and way in the distance Reeth stood proudly on the flanks of Calver Hill, bathed in golden sunshine. I was filled with a sense of well being. From that day I have visited every part of the Yorkshire Dales, read and collected as many books as possible and spent many happy holidays there. I was fortunate enough to study Geography at Lancaster University, which has given me a deeper understanding of the physical and human geography of the area. After graduating I started my career with Tetley's Brewery in Leeds where I was given an area to look after for six months as part of my training – I looked after all freehouses between Kettlewell and Hebden Bridge.

The idea of The Inn Way is to put this knowledge and love of the Yorkshire Dales into a walk so that people who wish to discover the Dales may do so with the assurance that they are seeing and experiencing the best the area has to offer. I marked on a map my favourite places including villages, viewpoints, castles, bridges and pubs and then joined them up to form a circular walk. The walk starts and finishes in Grassington, which is easily accessible and offers ample facilities and services, and will take six days to complete covering 76 miles. Eleven dales and twenty six inns are passed along the way, which serve ales from at least ten different breweries, as well as Roman roads and forts, haunted bridges and the Corpse Way, a medieval castle which held Mary Queen of Scots, Brigantes dikes, monastic roads and guideposts, nature reserves, waterfalls, lead mines, glacial lakes, breathtaking views and much, much more. The six stages are designed so they are between eleven and fourteen miles in length, and that you pass at least one pub at lunchtime and the overnight village has plenty of facilities.

PLAN OF THE BOOK

The Inn Way...to the Yorkshire Dales will take six days to complete either as a 76-mile circular walk or broken down into individual linear walks of up to fourteen miles. Each walk has its own section within this book, which is designed to provide all of the necessary information for that day's walk. These individual sections contain an information page, route description, hand-drawn map and a detailed compilation of information concerning places of interest along the way that are brought to life by a selection of fascinating short quotations from selected travel authors who have visited the Yorkshire Dales over the last hundred years or more.

Interpretation of Walk Information and Route Descriptions

Walk Information

Points of interest:	This provides a summary of the highlights of the day's walk.
Distance:	The distance travelled in a day has been broken down into 'morning' and 'afternoon' sections with a total mileage for the day. All distances given are 'map miles' estimated from Ordnance Survey (1:25,000) maps. All distances quoted are in miles and yards, conversions as follows: Yards to metres multiply by 0.9 Miles to kilometres multiply by 1.6 Kilometres to miles multiply by 0.6 Metres to yards multiply by 1.1
Time:	Total time taken to complete the day's walk. This is based upon a walking speed of two-and-a-half miles per hour with consideration for steep ascents, rest stops and viewpoints. This time does not include the obligatory hour lunch break!

Terrain:	Summary of the type of walking surface you will encounter along the way, for example stony tracks, long grass, boggy ground etc, as well as any particularly steep ascents or descents and exposed sections.
Ascents:	Each of the major climbs of the day are listed complete with maximum height gained. This figure is not necessarily the total amount of climbing to be done as most ascents start between 100 and 250 metres above sea level. All height figures are in metres (see conversion table above).
Viewpoints:	The most spectacular viewpoints are listed for each Stage - remember you camera as well as your binoculars!

Facilities

Inn	See list of 'Public Houses'
B&B	Bed and Breakfast accommodation available in the village.
Shop	At least one shop selling general provisions.
PO	Post Office, many of which sell limited provisions.
Café	Teas and light refreshments available.
Bus	Served by public transport, although services are often seasonal and infrequent.
Phone	Public payphone
Toilets	Public conveniences
Info	Tourist Information Centres or National Park Information Centres.
YH	Youth Hostel accommodation available in or near the village.
Camp	Campsite in or near the village.

ROUTE DESCRIPTIONS & RIGHTS OF WAY

Route Descriptions

The following abbreviations have been used throughout the route descriptions:

SP	Signpost	FB	Footbridge
FP	Footpath	YH	Youth Hostel
BW	Bridleway	Approx	Approximately

Due to the large numbers of visitors who visit the Yorkshire Dales National Park to enjoy various outdoor pursuits, route finding is relatively easy as most footpaths and bridleways are clearly marked, well maintained and used. The signposts are often colour-coded as follows: yellow for footpaths, blue for bridleways and red for byways. Often, the path on the ground is clearly defined and easy to follow, however, some sections cross more remote areas and high moorland where route finding may be more difficult, especially in bad weather. Always take up-to-date OS maps with you as well as a compass or GPS.

The route has been walked several times using solely the route descriptions given, however, to ensure ease of use they should be used in conjunction with the hand-drawn maps that appear within the text, with an OS map as back-up. Each route description has been divided into paragraphs that correspond with one of these detailed hand-drawn maps.

A reasonable walking speed is 3 mph, although this averages out to around 2.5 mph over the course of a day. With this in mind, it will take about 5 minutes to walk 0.25 miles, 10 minutes to walk 0.5 miles and 20 minutes to walk 1 mile.

Grid References

Grid References have been given within the Route Descriptions to assist route finding; for example the Grid Reference for Arncliffe Church is SD 933 719 and Bare House is SE 005 669.

Rights of Way

Public Rights of Way or Open Access areas must be used during the completion of this walk. The Inn Way only follows footpaths, bridleways, byways, Unclassified County Roads (UCR) and country lanes. On some occasions the path on the ground differs slightly from the Right of Way shown on the OS map. Where this occurs I have followed the path on the ground to avoid creating more paths and consequently more erosion.

The countryside is slowly but constantly evolving and changing; stiles may become bridle-gates, gates may disappear, paths may be re-surfaced, pubs or shops may close. Footpath repair and conservation work is an important and never ending job and occasionally Rights of Way may be altered or diverted to prevent further erosion damage or to simply improve the line of the footpath. Any changes and diversions will be clearly signposted and must be followed, and are usually marked on the most up-to-date Ordnance Survey maps. Feedback concerning these changes is always welcome, as this book is updated at each reprint.

Open Access

The Countryside and Rights of Way Act 2000 opened up 4,000 square miles of mountain, moor, heath, down and common land throughout England. Walkers can now freely roam across this Open Access land without having to stay on public footpaths. These new rights of access relate to mapped areas of access land that comprise predominantly of unenclosed areas of mountains, hills and moorland – not enclosed fields or private land – and are marked on Ordnance Survey maps as areas of yellow shading. On the ground, key access points display a brown circular Open Access symbol as well as local information. Generally, you can get onto Access Land via existing Rights of Way or moorland roads. Farmers and landowners can restrict access rights to their land for 28 days each year, for example during the breeding season. They may also apply for long term restrictions where necessary for land management, safety or fire prevention. Restrictions or closures are shown on the Countryside Access website or on local notices. Walkers using Open Access land have a responsibility to respect and protect the countryside and follow the Countryside Code.

Long sections of The Inn Way follow existing Rights of Way across Open Access land, primarily across the high, open fells. Always take your Ordnance Survey maps with you so you can take full advantage of this Open Access land.

For further information visit *www.openaccess.gov.uk*

THE MAPS

The sixteen hand-drawn maps are based upon the Ordnance Survey Explorer (1:25,000) series of maps and are designed to tie in with the route descriptions. The route is easy to follow and is marked by a series of dots along footpaths and bridleways or arrows along roads and tracks (see 'Key to Maps'). Landmarks, places of interest, hills and contours are also given to help you. These maps should guide you safely around *The Inn Way...to the Yorkshire Dales;* however, they do not show the surrounding countryside in detail.

Always take Ordnance Survey Explorer maps (scale 1:25,000) with you on your walk, as well as a compass or GPS.

Ordnance Survey Explorer Map OL2 (1:25,000)
'Yorkshire Dales Southern & Western areas'. This map covers lower Wharfedale from Kettlewell, lower Littondale and the environs of Grassington.

Ordnance Survey Explorer Map OL30 (1:25,000)
'Yorkshire Dales Northern & Central areas'. This map covers all of Swaledale, Wensleydale and Coverdale, as well as Upper Wharfedale and Littondale.

KEY TO THE MAPS

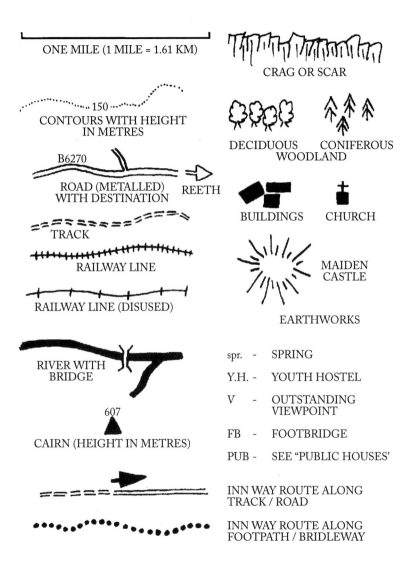

ONE MILE (1 MILE = 1.61 KM)

150
CONTOURS WITH HEIGHT
IN METRES

B6270

ROAD (METALLED)
WITH DESTINATION   REETH

TRACK

RAILWAY LINE

RAILWAY LINE (DISUSED)

RIVER WITH
BRIDGE

607
CAIRN (HEIGHT IN METRES)

CRAG OR SCAR

DECIDUOUS   CONIFEROUS
WOODLAND

BUILDINGS   CHURCH

MAIDEN
CASTLE

EARTHWORKS

spr. -   SPRING

Y.H. -   YOUTH HOSTEL

V   -   OUTSTANDING
VIEWPOINT

FB -   FOOTBRIDGE

PUB -   SEE "PUBLIC HOUSES'

INN WAY ROUTE ALONG
TRACK / ROAD

INN WAY ROUTE ALONG
FOOTPATH / BRIDLEWAY

SAFETY

• Never underestimate the strenuous nature of walking particularly when this is combined with high ground and the elements. Do not attempt to complete a walk that is beyond your skill, experience or level of fitness.

• Obtain a detailed weather forecast before setting out on your walk. If the weather turns bad then turn back the way you have walked. Conditions can change for the worse within minutes reducing visibility and making walking hazardous with cloud, mist, strong winds and rain all year round. The temperature, wind speed and general weather conditions on exposed moorland can vary significantly from the conditions in sheltered valleys.

• Take Ordnance Survey maps (1:25,000) of the area. It is essential to carry a compass or GPS (Global Positioning System) as some sections of this walk cross high fells or open moorland with few landmarks.

• Your boots are the most important thing; make sure that they are waterproof, comfortable and have good ankle support and sturdy soles. The wrong footwear can mean every step is blisteringly painful - and you will make over 26,000 strides on a 12-mile walk!

• Waterproof and windproof coat and trousers are essential as well as gloves, hat and fleece for warmth; there is no such thing as bad weather only the wrong clothes!

• Wear clothing made from synthetic fibres, which are quick drying and help 'wick' moisture away from the skin. Avoid cotton and jeans as these soak up moisture.

• Travel light as a heavy rucksack can tire you out, cause backache and make your shoulders sore. Take only essential items such as a change of clothes (remember that several thin layers will keep you warmer than thick bulky layers and take up less room), nourishing snack foods, basic first aid kit, blister plasters, hat, sun cream, whistle, water bottle (minimum 1 litre), torch, 'survival' bag and mobile 'phone. Line your rucksack with a large plastic bag to keep the contents dry.

- Drink plenty of fluids (not alcohol) and eat food regularly to keep energy levels up.

- Regularly check your location against the map and route description. Always look for at least three landmarks to confirm your location. If you become misplaced (or lost), re-trace your steps back to your last known location.

- Always walk in a group unless you are very experienced and inform someone of your intended route and report your safe arrival. If you are delayed but safe then make sure you let someone know so that the Mountain Rescue Team is not called out.

- Mobile phone coverage in the Yorkshire Dales is patchy due to the nature of the landscape, with reception limited to the high moors and fells as well as the larger villages and towns such as Grassington and Hawes. Many of the more remote valleys have no reception at all. In an emergency, go to the nearest village or farmhouse to use a phone.

- In an emergency in a remote and inaccessible location call out the Mountain Rescue Team by 'phoning 999 and asking for Mountain Rescue (via the Police), giving details of the incident and location. If you do not have a mobile 'phone then summon help with six blasts of your whistle. NB: Mountain Rescue is an Emergency Service

- Take care when crossing rivers or roads and walk in single file (facing oncoming traffic) when walking along country lanes. Do not explore old mine or quarry workings.

- When walking through grassy moorland areas keep a watchful eye for adders, Britain's only poisonous snake. Adders like south-facing slopes and can often be found basking in the sun. Adders will only bite if they are startled or scared - if you are unlucky enough to be bitten seek medical help immediately.

- Above all, keep your hands out of your pockets and look where you are going!

REMEMBER: "An experienced walker knows when to turn back"

COUNTRYSIDE CODE

Consider other people
Showing consideration and respect for other people makes the countryside a pleasant environment for everyone – at home, at work and at leisure.

Enjoy the countryside and respect its life and work
Do not touch crops, machinery or livestock. We have a responsibility to protect our countryside now and for future generations, so make sure you don't harm animals, birds, plants or trees. Wild animals and farm animals can behave unpredictably if you get too close, especially if they're with their young – so give them plenty of space. Tread gently – discover the beauty of the natural environment and take care not to damage, destroy or remove features such as rocks, plants and trees. They provide homes and food for wildlife, and add to everybody's enjoyment of the countryside.

Leave gates and property as you find them
Please respect the working life of the countryside, as our actions can affect people's livelihoods, our heritage, and the safety and welfare of animals and ourselves. Use stiles and gates to cross fences and walls and close gates behind you. When walking across fields with crops follow the paths wherever possible. Our heritage belongs to all of us – be careful not to disturb ruins and historic sites.

Keep to public Rights of Way or Open Access areas.
Footpaths are for walkers; bridleways are for cyclists, horse-riders and walkers. Motorbikes and cars should keep to roads.

Do not make excessive noise
The hills and valleys should be quiet places

Take care on country roads
Face oncoming traffic and walk in single file

Safeguard water supplies
Streams are used by livestock and often feed reservoirs for drinking supplies. Do not foul water supplies.

Guard against risk of fire
Uncontrolled fires can devastate grassy hillsides or moorland, which may never fully recover. Do not start fires or drop matches.

Keep dogs under control
A loose dog can be catastrophic for ground nesting birds, sheep and sometimes the dog itself. Your dog must be under control so that it does not disturb or scare farm animals or wildlife. By law, farmers are entitled to destroy a dog that injures or worries their animals. If a farm animal chases you and your dog, it is safer to let your dog off the lead – don't risk getting hurt by trying to protect it. Clear up after your dog and make sure your dog is wormed regularly.

Take litter home
Litter is dangerous and unsightly.

Safety
Weather can change quickly, are you fully equipped for the hills? You're responsible for your own safety and for others in your care, so be prepared for the unexpected; follow local advice and signs. Use up-to-date OS maps. Part of the appeal of the countryside is that you can get away from it all. You may not see anyone for hours and there are many places without mobile-phone signals, so let someone know where you're going and when you expect to return.

USEFUL INFORMATION

If you are travelling by public transport make sure that you check train and bus times before you set out as these often vary seasonally. Book accommodation in advance as B&Bs and Youth Hostels can get fully booked up during the summer months and may close temporarily during the winter months.

InnWay Publications Website: www.innway.co.uk
A comprehensive site with detailed information to help organise your walk.

Yorkshire Dales National Park Information Centres:
Aysgarth Falls Information Centre   01969 662910
Grassington Information Centre   01756 751690
Hawes Information Centre   01969 666210
Reeth Information Centre   01748 884059
National Park Information Centres offer in-depth local knowledge as well as fascinating interpretative displays of the history of the Yorkshire Dales, issues facing the area and Dales life in general through various forms of media. They also form a contact point for the Ranger Service and weather information.

Tourist Information Centres (TIC):
Harrogate   01423 537300
Leyburn   01969 623069
Richmond   01748 828742
Skipton   01756 792809

Weather Information
MetOffice Weathercall   09014 722 067
Information supplied by Met Office. Premium Rate calls.
Website: www.metoffice.gov.uk

Public Transport:
Public Transport Traveline: 0871 200 22 33
A 'one stop' information line for national, regional and local bus and train services.
Website: www.traveline.org.uk

National Express bookings   08717 818181
Rail Enquiries   08457 484950
The nearest railway station to Grassington is at Skipton.

Baggage Courier Service:
Brigantes Baggage Courier   01729 830463
Mr J. M. Schofield
Rookery Cottage
Kirkby Malham
Skipton
North Yorkshire
BD23 4BX
Website: www.brigantesenglishwalks.com

Organisations:
Campaign for Real Ale CAMRA   01727 867201
230 Hatfield Road
St Albans
Hertfordshire
Website: www.camra.org.uk

Rambler's Association   020 7339 8500
2nd Floor, Camelford House
87 - 90 Albert Embankment
London, SE17TW
Website: www.ramblers.org.uk

North Yorkshire County Council   01609 780780
County Hall
Northallerton
DL7 8AD
Website: www.northyorks.gov.uk

Yorkshire Dales National Park Authority 0870 1 666333
Hebden Road
Grassington
North Yorkshire
Website: www.yorkshiredales.org.uk

Welcome to Yorkshire   0113 322 3500
Dry Sand Foundry
Foundry Square,
Leeds
Website: www.yorkshire.com

Youth Hostel Association   0870 870 8808
Trevelyan House
Dimple Road
Matlock
Derbyshire
Youth Hostels are located at Grinton (near Reeth) and Kettlewell.
Website: www.yha.org.uk

For a detailed accommodation guide send a Stamped Addressed Envelope to:
InnWay Publications, 102 Leeds Road, Harrogate HG2 8HB.

John A. Ives

FACILITIES PROVIDED AT EACH OF THE OVERNIGHT STOPS

Stage One - Grassington

Grassington serves as the starting and finishing point because it is easy to get to and has plenty of facilities. It is an attractive small town set amongst the rolling hills of Upper Wharfedale, a popular tourist destination due to its picturesque cobbled square, stone cottages and winding alleyways. Situated near the south-eastern corner of the National Park boundary, Grassington is the 'gateway' to the high fells and sweeping valleys of the southern Yorkshire Dales.

How to get there:
By public transport - the nearest train station is at Skipton, from where there are frequent bus services to Grassington.

By car - Skipton is reached via the A65 from Leeds, A650 from Bradford or the A59 from Harrogate to the east or Preston from the west. The B6265 heads north from Skipton directly to Grassington. There is limited long stay parking available at Grassington, so please make use of the public transport network and save time, money, hassle and the environment! There is a large 'pay & display' car park in the village operated by the Yorkshire Dales National Park Authority; ask in the Information Centre about details of long stay parking. Hotels, pubs and Bed & Breakfast providers usually allow you to leave your car with them if you stay with them at the start and finish of your walk - always 'phone to check.

Facilities - Grassington is a thriving Dales town, known locally as the 'capital of Upper Wharfedale'. Here you will find a good selection of shops, facilities and amenities including Barclays Bank (cashpoint), outdoor pursuits shop, small supermarket, general stores, Post Office, craft shops, fish & chip shop, restaurants, cafés, delicatessen, bookshop, Off Licence, newsagents, hardware shop, garage, police station, doctors' surgery, chemist, telephones, toilets, Upper Wharfedale Folk Museum, bus service, car park (limited long stay, headquarters of the Upper Wharfedale Fell Rescue Association and a good selection of hotels, pubs and bed and breakfasts.

The National Park Information Centre at Grassington has details of local events, services, facilities and accommodation. Maps, books and literature associated with the Yorkshire Dales are available. It houses a display area which provides a fascinating insight into the influences behind the geography, geology and landscape of the Dales and also illustrates how the National Park is managed to try to strike a balance between conservation, recreational use and the people who live and work in the Dales.

Stage Two - Buckden

Buckden offers bed and breakfasts, general stores, tea rooms, restaurant, telephone, toilets, bus service, large car park, National Trust Information Barn (Town Head Barn) and the Buck Inn.

Stage Three - Askrigg

Askrigg offers hotel accommodation, bed & breakfasts, restaurant, general stores, florist, café, outdoor pursuits centre, bus service, toilets, telephone and three pubs.

Stage Four - Reeth

Reeth offers numerous bed and breakfasts, hotel accommodation, restaurant, tea rooms, ice cream parlour, craft and gift shops, Post Office, bakery, general stores, bookshop, newsagent, garage, travelling fish & chip van (Fridays), bus service, doctors' surgery, Swaledale Folk Museum, National Park Information Centre, Youth Hostel (Grinton), toilets, telephone, campsite and three pubs.

Stage Five - West Burton

West Burton offers bed & breakfasts, Post Office and general store, tea rooms, butcher, craft shop, telephone, bus service and the Fox & Hounds.

Stage Six - Kettlewell

Kettlewell offers several bed and breakfasts, cafés, bistro, general stores, Post Office, Youth Hostel, craft shop, outdoor pursuits shop, toilets, telephone, garage, campsite, bus service, car park and three pubs.

All of the above information is for guide purposes only and many facilities are liable to change. If it is important - check it.

PUBLIC HOUSES

The classic Dales' inn... stone-flagged floor, low oak beams, cosy corners, open fire and hand-pulled Yorkshire ale; there really is no where better to recuperate after a long day on the fells. The route of The Inn Way...to the Yorkshire Dales is designed to take in as many of these pubs as possible, including a number of pubs that have remained totally unchanged for many decades. All pubs encountered along the route have been listed - I'll let you make up your own mind as to your favourite ones. NB: If you are relying on a pub for lunchtime food then 'phone to check opening times.

1. *Black Horse Hotel, Garrs Lane, Grassington: 01756 752770*
   Set back from the cobbled square, this imposing whitewashed old coaching inn offers a warm welcome with a log fire set in a large open fireplace and a good range of real ales.
   ACC / FOOD / GDN / FIRE / TRAD

2. *Devonshire Hotel, Main Street, Grassington: 01756 752525*
   This beautiful old stone-built coaching inn dominates the cobbled square. Inside, the lounge bar is comfortably furnished with some cosy corners whilst there is also a separate dining room, both of which are busy with locals, walkers and visitors. It is named after the Duke of Devonshire who was instrumental in the development of the local lead mines and who still owns large tracts of Wharfedale.
   ACC / FOOD / GDN / FIRE / TRAD

3. *Foresters Arms, Main Street, Grassington: 01756 752349*
   Set in the heart of Grassington this pub is the village 'local'; the pub has been run by the same family for over 35 years. Separate rooms and a games room ensure that this pub is full of atmosphere and is a popular meeting place. It also serves an excellent pint of beer.
   ACC / FOOD / GDN / FIRE / TRAD / BAR

4. *Tennant Arms, Kilnsey: 01756 752301*
   This 17th Century coaching inn has a spectacular setting with Kilnsey Crag dominating the scene.
   ACC / FOOD / GDN / TRAD / FIRE / BAR / INN

5. *Falcon Inn, Arncliffe: 01756 770205*
When you walk into this pub you step back in time; wooden bench seating, several small rooms, outside loos and beer straight from the cask served from a porcelain jug. One of England's classic country pubs – a visit to this beautiful old hostelry is a must.
ACC / FOOD / GDN / TRAD / FIRE / BAR / INN

6. *Queens Arms, Litton: 01756 770208*
Lovely old Dales pub with oak beams, exposed stonework, stone-flagged floors and open fires. Beautiful setting at the foot of Old Cote Moor and Horse Head Moor, with unsurpassed views across Littondale towards Pen-y-ghent at the head of the valley. The home of Litton Ale, which is brewed on the premises.
ACC / FOOD / GDN / TRAD / FIRE / BAR / INN

7. *Buck Inn, Buckden: 01756 760228*
This imposing building in the heart of the village operates as a busy hotel, restaurant and pub. The small stone-flagged bar area retains a great deal of character with an open fire and a good range of real ales on offer. Benches at the front of this stone inn afford superb views across Wharfedale towards the soaring heights of Birks Fell, which you have just walked over!
ACC / FOOD / GDN / TRAD / FIRE / BAR

8. *White Lion, Cray: 01756 760262*
There is not much to Cray, a farm or two and the pub, but its setting amongst waterfalls and the surrounding wild moorland is superb. The White Lion is a classic example of a traditional Dales inn, with a delightful stone-flagged bar complete with beamed ceiling and large fireplace. There is also a raised snug area as well as a small dining room. Note the 'ring the bull' by the door – a rare example of this old pub game.
ACC / FOOD / GDN / TRAD / FIRE / BAR / INN

9. *Rose and Crown, Bainbridge: 01969 650225*
This pub dates back to 1445, although it was much altered in the 19th Century, and has been providing hospitality for travellers for centuries. The Bainbridge Forest Horn hangs in the passage-way; the horn was blown during the winter months to guide people through the forest of Wensleydale, a tradition that continues today.
ACC / FOOD / GDN / TRAD / FIRE / BAR / INN

10. *Victoria Arms, Worton: 01969 650314*
This unassuming small pub is situated along the main A684 but a
closer look will reveal an unspoilt Dales local. This is one of the last
surviving examples in England of a time when most landlords of
country inns would also have a smallholding. The landlord keeps a flock
of sheep as well as a good pint! The walls are full of fascinating bric-a-
brac, but watch out for the back-end of the stuffed fox!
TRAD / FIRE / BAR / INN

11. *King's Arms Hotel, Askrigg: 01969 650258*
This wonderful 18th Century building was originally built as a manor
house but later developed into a coaching inn; Turner once stayed here
whilst painting in the Dales. It is a pub of great character with wood
panelling, an inglenook fireplace and old saddle hooks hanging from the
ceiling. The pub was used as the 'Drover's Arms' in the BBC TV series
'All Creatures Great and Small'.
FOOD / GDN / TRAD / FIRE / BAR / INN

12. *Crown Inn, Askrigg: 01969 650298*
This unpretentious pub has a warm, friendly atmosphere and offers
everything a traditional village local should. An old cast iron range
warms one of the small snug areas, whilst locals play darts in another. It
has a good reputation for its home-made food.
FOOD / GDN / TRAD / FIRE / BAR / INN

Addendum – White Rose Hotel, Askrigg: 01969 650515
Situated along Askrigg's sweeping main street, this large elegant hotel
was built in the 1830s originally as a private house. Inside, there is a
traditional bar, a large restaurant and conservatory as well as a sheltered
beer garden to the rear.
ACC / FOOD / GDN / TRAD

13. *King's Head, Gunnerside: 01748 886261*
This stone-built pub is situated close to the bridge over Gunnerside Beck
in the heart of the village and dates back to the 17th Century when it was
a blacksmith's shop and alehouse. The cosy bar is dominated by a large
stone fireplace which, coupled with the wholesome food and friendly
atmosphere, makes you want to stay all afternoon.
FOOD / GDN / TRAD / FIRE / BAR / INN

14. *The Black Bull, Reeth: 01748 884213*

Overlooking the green, this old coaching inn dates back to 1680 and is a prominent landmark with its three-storey whitewashed facade. The pub retains a great deal of character with slanting doorways, stone-flagged floors, low beams and large open fireplace set in a cosy bar area that was used in a scene from a James Herriot film. The bow-fronted window of the restaurant once belonged to a Georgian draper's shop. Note the upside-down pub sign, the result of a long running planning dispute with the National Park Authority a number of years ago.

ACC / FOOD / GDN / TRAD / FIRE / BAR / INN

15. *King's Arms, Reeth: 01748 884259*

This impressive Georgian building is known locally as the Middle House. The bar is comfortable with a lively, local atmosphere and is warmed by a huge inglenook fireplace, one of the finest in the Yorkshire Dales. Outside, you can enjoy a quiet drink sat around a table on the old marketplace cobblestones.

ACC / FOOD / GDN / TRAD / FIRE / INN

16. *Buck Hotel, Reeth: 01748 884210*

Situated at the junction of the Swaledale and Arkengarthdale roads, this imposing old coaching inn looks out across the large sloping green. Inside, the spacious bar boasts large beams and an open fire.

ACC / FOOD / GDN / TRAD / FIRE

17. *Bridge Hotel, Grinton: 01748 884224*

This stone built inn is aptly named for it is situated between Grinton Bridge that spans the River Swale and the smaller bridge over Grinton Gill. The interior is divided into three rooms on various levels warmed by open fires, including a comfortable bar, large dining room and games room. It boasts a warm and friendly atmosphere where walkers are most welcome.

ACC / FOOD / GDN / TRAD / FIRE / INN

18. *Wheatsheaf Hotel, Carperby: 01969 663216*

Several small rooms help create a cosy atmosphere; the real life James Herriot had his honeymoon break here in 1941, and Henry Hall and Greta Garbo stayed here in 1942, signing the guestbook "Great Garbo, Hollywood." Inside, there is a residents' lounge complete with inglenook fireplace, dining room, lounge bar and a cosy snug.

ACC / FOOD / GDN / TRAD / FIRE

19. *Palmer Flatt Hotel, Aysgarth Falls: 01969 663228*
Situated above the famous Aysgarth Falls on the main Leyburn to Hawes road, this 18th Century hotel stands on the foundations of a medieval hospice for pilgrims returning from the Holy Land in the time of the Crusades, its unusual name comes from the palm branches brought back by these pilgrims. The interior is spacious and furnished in a traditional style.
ACC / FOOD / GDN / TRAD / FIRE

20. *Fox and Hounds, West Burton: 01969 663111*
A lovely small inn offering excellent local ales in a comfortable bar with extensive views over the spacious village green; probably the best beer garden in the world!
ACC / FOOD / GDN / TRAD / FIRE / INN

21. *Thwaite Arms, Horsehouse: 01969 640206*
A wonderful stone-built Dales pub with a cobbled and flagged forecourt, several small rooms inside with stone-flagged floors, bench seating and open fires. One of the most remote pubs in the Yorkshire Dales, surrounded by spectacular scenery. A classic example of an unspoilt country inn.
ACC / FOOD / GDN / TRAD / FIRE / BAR / INN

22. *King's Head, Kettlewell: 01756 760242*
Tucked away in the heart of the village, this pub attracts a mixture of locals, visitors and walkers. It is a pub of great character with stone-flagged floors, beams and a superb inglenook fireplace dominating the bar – the perfect place to dry out after the long walk from West Burton as you can actually sit in the fireplace!
ACC / FOOD / GDN / TRAD / FIRE / BAR / INN

23. *Blue Bell Hotel, Kettlewell: 01756 760230*
This attractive whitewashed inn dates back to 1680 and was once a coaching inn on the London to Richmond stagecoach route; the pub is named after an old stagecoach company. The interior retains a traditional bar area warmed by a roaring fire, as well as several small dining areas. Watch the world go by from the benches at the front.
ACC / FOOD / GDN / TRAD / FIRE / BAR / INN

24 *Racehorses Hotel, Kettlewell: 01756 760233*

This large hotel is situated directly opposite the Blue Bell and was once used as the stables – the name is reminiscent of the stagecoach days as the 'trace horses' were used to pull the coaches up the steep Park Rash Pass behind the village. The comfortable interior is divided into several rooms with some lovely old stone fireplaces.

ACC / FOOD / GDN / TRAD / FIRE

25. *Clarendon Hotel, Hebden: 01756 752446*

This large Victorian stone-built pub is set back from the main Grassington to Pateley Bridge road in the heart of Hebden. This unpretentious village local has a good reputation for food, well-kept ales and a warm welcome.

ACC / FOOD / GDN / TRAD / FIRE

26. *Fountaine Inn, Linton: 01756 752210*

This beautiful old inn boasts a lovely setting overlooking the delightful village green through which flows a small stream spanned by a variety of bridges. The interior retains a great deal of character with small rooms, low ceilings and open fires. Good reputation for food.

FOOD / GDN / TRAD / FIRE / BAR / INN

KEY
· ·

ACC	Accommodation
FOOD	Meals available
GDN	Beer garden (includes lawns, patios and outside benches)
TRAD	Cask ales available (Real Ale)
FIRE	Open fires
BAR	Traditional public bar area often with stone-flagged floor.
INN	Classic country inn

THE BREWERIES

Good pubs and Real Ale are both in plentiful supply throughout the Yorkshire Dales with a wide range of good quality locally-brewed ales on offer. Yorkshire is noted for its bitter ales, often full-flavoured and rich in colour with a pronounced hoppy aroma.

Great Britain is renowned throughout the world for its beer, with literally hundreds of breweries producing thousands of different beers, each with their own distinctive character, flavour, strength and heritage! Well-loved local breweries play an important role in the strong regional identities of this country, with many producing specific styles of beers to suit local palates. With this in mind, I have only listed independent local or regional breweries whose beers reflect the region in which they are sold, rather than national or international brewers who often concentrate on brand image and profit at the expense of regional identity.

Many pubs, inns and hotels throughout the Yorkshire Dales are free houses, with a handful of tenanted and managed houses in the larger villages and towns. This means that the licensees are free to choose whichever brand he or she likes, however, in reality trade deals and discounts often dictate which products an outlet sells, although the now common 'guest beer' adds variety, all of which means that you may find a whole range of beers on sale that are not listed below.

INDEPENDENT REGIONAL BREWERS

Black Sheep Brewery
Wellgarth, Masham, North Yorkshire
This independent brewery was set up in 1992 by Paul Theakston following the take-over in 1987 of his old family firm by Scottish and Newcastle Breweries, as they were then known. The brewery is situated in the former Lightfoot Brewery maltings literally next door to the old offices of T&R Theakston Ltd; Lightfoot's were Masham's 'other' brewery, purchased by Theakston's in 1919. Black Sheep Brewery produces a range of traditional Yorkshire 'style' beers using

only the finest ingredients and traditional brewing plant rescued from Hartley's of Ulverston. The pronounced bitterness and characteristic flavour of the beers is reminiscent of some of the old West Riding brews, mainly due to the fact that traditional Yorkshire Square fermenting vessels are used. In spring 2004, a second brewhouse was installed to run in parallel with their existing brewhouse, which has almost doubled capacity to around 80,000 barrels a year. Black Sheep Brewery only supply to the free trade on a rapidly increasing geographical basis. Black Sheep Ale is a superb example of a Yorkshire strong ale and well worth sampling if you come across it.

Cask ales available include Best Bitter (ABV 3.8%), Black Sheep Ale (ABV 4.4%) and Riggwelter (ABV 5.9%).

Copper Dragon Brewery
Keighley Road, Skipton, North Yorkshire

Copper Dragon Brewery was established in the Yorkshire Dales market town of Skipton back in 2002, a century since Scott's Skipton Brewery - the town's last brewery - closed. They have drawn on this brewing heritage to create a distinctive range of cask-conditioned beers, including a number of brews using original Victorian recipes including Black Gold. The beers are brewed in a purpose-built German-style steam powered brewhouse. Such was the response to this new range of local ales that the brewery has expanded rapidly with outlets throughout the North of England, as well as a handful of brewery-owned pubs in the Skipton area including the Blue Bell Inn at Kettlewell.

Cask ales available include Black Gold (ABV 3.7%), Best Bitter (ABV 3.8%), Golden Pippin (ABV 3.9%), Scotts 1816 (ABV 4.1%), Challenger IPA (ABV 4.4%).

Dent Brewery
Cowgill, Dentdale, Cumbria

Small brewery set up in 1990 in the Yorkshire Dales, although Dentdale actually falls within the boundaries of Cumbria. These fine ales are brewed using Dales spring water in a converted stone-built barn situated on a hillside in the upper reaches of Dentdale, which makes this one of the most remote breweries in the country. The brewery produces a wide range of award-winning ales. *Cask ales available include Bitter (ABV 3.7%), Aviator (ABV 4%), Rambrau (ABV 4.5%), Ramsbottom Strong Ale (ABV 4.5%), Kamikaze (ABV 5%) and T'owd Tup (ABV 6%).*

Jennings Brothers
The Castle Brewery, Cockermouth, Cumbria

Jennings is Cumbria's only remaining regional brewer, first established in 1828 with brewing taking place at the Castle Brewery since 1874. In 2005 Jennings became part of the Wolverhampton & Dudley Breweries group, now known as Marston's PLC, which is one of the UK's largest independent brewers and pub operators who also acquired Marston's Brewery in 1999. A superb selection of real ales is supplied to their estate of around 130 pubs and over 300 free trade accounts. Jennings' heartland is the old county of Cumberland, however, recent acquisitions and new free trade accounts have expanded their trading area into Yorkshire, Lancashire and the North East. Cumberland Ale is particularly satisfying after a long day's walk. *Cask ales available include Mild (ABV 3.1%), Bitter (ABV 3.5%), Cumberland Ale (ABV 4%), Cocker Hoop (ABV 4.6%), Sneck Lifter (ABV 5.1%) plus seasonal ales well worth looking out for.*

Litton Ale Brewery
Queens Arms, Litton, North Yorkshire

This small brewery was founded in 2003 at the Queen's Arms at Litton, set in the beautiful upper reaches of Littondale. Brewed using pure spring water from the hillside behind the pub, their range of full flavoured ales can be sampled at the Queen's Arms as well as many more freehouses in the local area. *Cask ales available include Litton Ale (ABV 3.8%), Leading Light (ABV 3.8%), Gold Crest (ABV 3.9%), Dark Star (ABV 4.0%), Potts Beck (ABV 4.2%).*

Timothy Taylor & Co.

Knowle Spring Brewery, Keighley, West Yorkshire

This famous independent Yorkshire brewery dates back to 1858 when Timothy Taylor began brewing in Cook Lane, Keighley. Demand for his quality ales was so great that in 1863 he moved to the Knowle Spring Brewery, which is still their home. A commitment to producing quality ales using the finest ingredients coupled with traditional brewing methods has paid dividends; indeed they still use Pennine spring water drawn from their own well as the 'liquor' for their award-winning ales. Landlord Pale Ale has won more awards nationally than any other beer and was judged to be the CAMRA Supreme Champion Beer of Britain in 1999 for a record third time. Taylor's brews are characterised by a pronounced bitterness with a distinctive almost floral 'hoppy' taste - the 'Taylor's Taste'. They also brew Golden Best, the last of the Pennine light milds.

Cask ales available include Dark Mild (ABV 3.5%), Golden Best (ABV 3.5%), Porter (ABV 3.8%), Best Bitter (ABV 4%), Landlord (ABV 4.3%), Ram Tam (ABV 4.3%).

T & R Theakston Ltd

Wellgarth, Masham, North Yorkshire

Established in 1827 in the small Dales town of Masham in lower Wensleydale, this brewery became part of Scottish and Newcastle Breweries, as they were then known, back in 1987. Theakston's ales were then promoted on a national basis, so much so that this once small country brewer became a household name synonymous with Real Ale; indeed, to cope with demand much of the production took place at Scottish Courage's Tyne Brewery. Rather surprisingly, the small Masham brewery remained open producing a limited amount of beer, with a great deal of emphasis placed upon the traditional qualities of the Theakston's brand with its working cooper's shop and picturesque stone-built brewery. Even more surprisingly, the Masham brewery and the Theakston beer brands were sold back to members of the Theakston family in autumn 2003, making this famous and highly regarded traditional brewer once again an independent family-run business. Their most famous brand is the award-winning

Theakston's Old Peculier, a legendary strong Yorkshire ale packed full of flavour - drink it with respect!

Cask ales available include Mild (ABV 3.5%), Best Bitter (ABV 3.8%), Black Bull Bitter (ABV 3.9%), XB (ABV 4.5%), Old Peculier (ABV 5.6%), as well as a range of seasonal ales.

Yorkshire Dales Brewing Co
Askrigg, North Yorkshire

Founded in 2005, this small brewery is housed in a converted milking parlour in the village of Askrigg in the heart of the Yorkshire Dales. A wide range of full flavoured ales are produced for local pubs, as well as freehouses throughout the North of England, all of which boast striking pump-clips. The names of the ales have strong links with the Dales, with many named after nearby hills and landmarks. Butter Tubs is a great example of a pale ale with its light golden colour, dry bitter taste and crisp citrus finish.

Cask ales available include Butter Tubs (ABV 3.7%), Booze Moor (ABV 3.8%), Buckden Pike (ABV 3.9%), Herriot Country Ale (ABV 4.0%), Askrigg Ale (ABV 4.3%), Yorkshire Penny (ABV 4.5%), plus a range of seasonal ales.

THE HISTORY OF THE DALES

It has taken 300 million years for the landforms of the Yorkshire Dales to take shape, yet less than 10,000 years for humans to manipulate this landscape. The landscape, land use and settlement pattern we see today is the result many varying influences that have taken place predominantly over the last 2,000 years. The first inhabitants of the Yorkshire Dales came after the retreat of the glaciers and subsequent warming of the climate, these were the Stone Age hunter-gatherers who lived in cave dwellings some 9,000 years ago, for example Elbolton Cave at Thorpe in Wharfedale. By around 1,300 BC flint tools were replaced by metal and this heralded the onset of the Bronze Age, however it was not until around 100 BC that man really made an impact on the landscape with the use of iron implements. The people of this Iron Age period were groups of tribes, predominantly Brigantes, collectively known as Celts. They settled and cultivated the land, favouring the well drained limestone areas because of the wet climate, and they built forts and defensive ditches. The shapes of their dwellings, square fields, burial circles and mounds can still be seen, indeed over 200 prehistoric sites have been identified within the Yorkshire Dales including the impressive Lea Green prehistoric settlement above Grassington and Tor Dyke above Kettlewell. These ancient British tribes lived in the Dales right through the Roman occupation.

The Romans came to Britain in AD 43 and had little trouble overcoming the Celtic tribes. They set up forts and towns linked together by straight roads and established a sophisticated social structure. They saw the Dales as an inhospitable land and left it to the native Celtic population, although they did exploit the mineral deposits in the area notably lead from Swaledale and Wharfedale. Forts were established around the Dales at Greta Bridge, Brough, Bowes, Ilkley and Elslack and these were connected by several roads which divided the area into a series of blocks. A fort was established in the very heart of the Yorkshire Dales at Bainbridge and this was almost continually manned from AD 80 to AD 400 with a garrison of

500 men. Traces of this fort can still be found on Brough Hill, and the route of a Roman road can be clearly seen cutting a straight course across the flanks of Wether Fell. The Roman occupation ended in AD 409, however, the now integrated Romano-British people continued to live in this area much as they had done before the end of Roman rule for another two centuries.

The next wave of settlers were the Angles from northern Germany in the 7th Century. They moved into the lower reaches of the Dales from the Vale of York and cleared woodland to make way for small farming communities. They brought with them a new language, culture and system of agriculture and the settlement pattern we see today was largely established by these Anglian farmers. Place names ending in 'ley', 'ton' and 'ham' indicate Anglian settlements. Danish settlers came next and in-filled between Anglian villages, their settlements are indicated by 'by' and 'thorpe'. The Norsemen came across from the east of Ireland in the tenth century and settled in the Lake District and the upper reaches of the Yorkshire Dales, particularly Swaledale above Gunnerside, Wensleydale above Bainbridge, Wharfedale above Buckden and most of Arkengarthdale. The landscape reminded them of their home back in Norway; hills, mountains and narrow valleys with sparse woodland. These Norse settlers did not like to live in communities but preferred single homesteads which complemented their style of pastoral farming. Places such as Keld, Muker and Gunnerside would have started as single Norse farms only developing into sizeable communities when the lead mines were developed. They grazed their livestock in the valleys during spring and autumn then moved them to the upland pastures over the summer months, leaving the grass to grow in the valley for use as winter fodder. These areas of upland grazing were known as 'saetrs' which can be seen today in the place names of the upper Dales, for example Gunnerside, Marsett and Countersett. Another common name is 'thwaite' which meant a clearing in woodland in Old Norse, for example Yockenthwaite in Langstrothdale. There are few physical remains of this period although the Norse language still remains today in the form of the old

Dales dialect with words such as dale, fell, beck, crag, gill, scar, tarn, mere and garth. So, the settlement pattern we see today was largely in place by the tenth century following the colonisation of the area by Anglo-Saxons, Danes and Norsemen.

Following the Norman Conquest in 1066, large tracts of land in the Yorkshire Dales were set aside as hunting preserves for the Lords of Richmond, Middleham and Skipton castles. Villages on the forest edge were developed as foresters' villages, notably Buckden, Bainbridge and Healaugh and a form of conservation was given to these hunting preserves, known as 'chases' (from the Norman-French word chasser 'to hunt') so that deer, boar and otter were protected. Apart from the hunting forests the Norman influence on the landscape was limited; by far the greatest influencing factor on land use in the Dales was from the monasteries. Fountains Abbey was founded in 1132, Jervaulx in 1145 and smaller priories were established at Coverham, Bolton, Easby, Ellerton and Marrick. Vast tracts of land were given to the monasteries by the Norman lords to ensure a safe passage to the next world. Fountains Abbey was by far the largest landowner with a million acres of grazing land throughout the North of England, and at the height of their power almost all of the area which now comes under the boundaries of the Yorkshire Dales National Park was controlled by monasteries. They brought with them excellent farming and sheep breeding skills and successfully ran these large grazing lands through a series of granges which were farms and chapels combined; the name 'grange' and 'cote' indicate the site of a former monastic farm. The grange which controlled the Craven district was at Kilnsey. A series of tracks were constructed which connected granges, abbeys and grazing lands. Many tracks remain today as green lanes, for example Mastiles Lane that runs westwards from Kilnsey across Malham Moor, although this famous green lane originally connected Fountains Abbey with the Lake District. Although wool was the main source of their wealth, the monastic houses of the Yorkshire Dales also developed lead mining, horse breeding, cheese-making, brewing, milling and fishing. They also drained marshy land, cleared woods and scrubland and built some of the earliest walls which were used mainly to keep unwanted animals out. The monks were entrepreneurs way ahead of their time who changed the way farming was carried out in this country. Following the Dissolution of the Monasteries and subsequent land ownership changes between 1537 and 1540, improvements in farming techniques continued especially with the enclosure of crofts around villages and farms. Prosperity improved and thus followed a period of house building throughout the Dales from 1670 to 1750.

Almost all of the drystone walls and enclosures we see today were constructed after Acts of Parliament between 1780 and 1820 when common village land was enclosed into rectangular fields thus improving land management. The upland areas were enclosed during the middle of the 19th Century. These fields were planned on paper and can be clearly identified by their straight lines across the hillside; earlier walls can be identified by their curving shapes. There are hundreds of miles of stone walls in the Yorkshire Dales, the construction of which was an enormous task; one waller could complete six metres of wall in a day. More recently, lead mining in the 19th Century has left a legacy of shafts, tunnels, spoil heaps and miners' cottages whilst tourism throughout the 20th Century and into the 21st Century has had a profound effect on the landscape of the Yorkshire Dales with car parks, holiday homes, caravan sites and traffic jams. There has also been a dramatic change in agriculture as farms have amalgamated, walls and hedgerows disappeared and traditional farming techniques all but gone. Threatened by these various pressures during the early 20th Century, the time was right to safeguard and manage this precious landscape.

The Yorkshire Dales National Park was designated in 1954 and covers 680 square miles of diverse landscape, ranging from the sweeping valleys and high moorland in the north and east of the National Park to the famed Three Peaks in the south-west and spectacular limestone pavements, gorges and caves in the south. It is, however, the sweeping valleys which are the true glory of the Yorkshire Dales. The underlying rocks give each valley a continuity of character, but they all have their own distinctive atmosphere from the wild upper reaches of Swaledale to the broad pastoral acres of Wensleydale. It must be stressed that the Yorkshire Dales National Park is neither national nor a park; 99% of the land within its boundaries is privately owned either by individual farmers or large landowners, such as water companies or shooting estates.

The Yorkshire Dales National Park Authority is responsible for the management of the National Park offering advice and assistance to local people and visitors, as well as acting as a local planning authority. It has two main purposes:

1. Conserve and enhance the natural beauty, wildlife and cultural heritage of the national Park.

2. Promote opportunities for public enjoyment and understanding of the special qualities of the National Park.

They also have a duty to foster the social and economic wellbeing of local communities.

A very difficult task indeed – it is hard to promote and conserve at the same time! Over 8 million people visit the Yorkshire Dales National Park annually, which is quite a burden for the 19,000 residents who live within its boundaries. Tourism is now the mainstay of the economy, bringing with it much needed income and jobs – many villages would not have their pub or shop if it were not for these visitors. However, tourism also brings challenges.

The Yorkshire Dales is undoubtedly one of England's most treasured landscapes, with deep valleys hemmed in by wild fells and rolling moorland. These valleys are drained by fast-flowing rivers and streams, which often cascade down spectacular waterfalls, whilst along the valley floor traditional hay-meadows add a mosaic of colour amongst green fields during late spring. It is not just the landscape that makes the Yorkshire Dales so special, but the people who have lived and worked in these valleys for generations, shaping its character over thousands of years from prehistoric times to the present day. Their legacy is all around from the 5,400 miles of drystone walls that criss-cross the dales and fells to the crumbling lead mines, ancient churches, Viking place-names and even the local accent. And this legacy lives on in the working hill-farms, buzzing village pubs, thriving local craft workshops and, most importantly, in the warm, spirited people of the Dales. An amazing 29% of the National Park is designated as Sites of Special Scientific Interest by Natural England due to the rare and threatened habitats. Many people come to the Yorkshire Dales to walk for it offers unrivalled terrain ranging from delightful riverside paths to challenging routes up the summits of the high fells. The Yorkshire Dales is blessed with an extensive right of way network with around 2,100 km of footpaths and bridleways as well as large areas of Open Access land that cover almost two-thirds of the National Park.

The Yorkshire Dales National Park Authority is now focussing much more on sustainable tourism and development to ensure a viable future for the area. The well-being of the local economy is inter-linked with conservation and public enjoyment. The National Park is a living landscape and there is a mutual dependence between the landscape, environment, local community and rural economy; the only way forward to ensure that this wonderful landscape is preserved and enhanced for future generations is through sustainable development and growth. By spending six days walking through the heart of the Yorkshire Dales, staying overnight in local inns and B&Bs, buying food and provisions en route, taking only memories and leaving only footprints, you are making a positive contribution to the upkeep of the Yorkshire Dales in a sustainable way. In addition to this, a percentage of the profit from the sale of this book will be donated to local conservation projects within the Yorkshire Dales National Park.

THE GEOLOGY OF THE DALES

The Yorkshire Dales is famous for its beautiful and awe-inspiring scenery, such as Kilnsey Crag, Malham Cove, Brimham Rocks or Aysgarth Falls. When you stand and admire these 'wonders of nature' you are actually looking at the result of millions of years of geological processes. The geology of the Dales is extremely complex; however, three distinct areas can be identified. The area centred around Ingleborough, Malham and Grassington is dominated by Great Scar Limestone with characteristic features such as limestone pavements, potholes, crags, scars and caves. To the north of this area, including Upper Wharfedale, Wensleydale and Swaledale, are the Yoredale series of rocks which are made up of layers of limestone, sandstone and shale sandwiched together. In many places the weaker shales and sandstones have become eroded exposing limestone ledges over which waterfalls cascade, this limestone can also be seen as rock terraces along the valley sides. To the south of the Great Scar Limestone the area is dominated by sandstones which are often weathered into weird and wonderful shapes, for example Brimham Rocks in Nidderdale.

300 million years ago a warm, shallow sea washed across what is now the Yorkshire Dales. This sea was teeming with marine life and as a result billions of tiny shells were deposited on the sea bed and compressed together to form a thick layer of limestone. As this ancient sea advanced and retreated sand and mud deposits were laid down by rivers draining into the sea thus creating layers of sandstone, shale and limestone on top of the Great Scar Limestone. These three types of rock form the basis of the Yorkshire Dales scenery. These rocks have been folded, uplifted and fractured through the movement of the earth's crust over millions of years. The result of these movements are the mountains, peaks and hills of the Pennines, fault lines such as the Craven Fault and mineral deposits such as lead.

This landscape has been modified by the effects of ice and water, especially during the series of Ice Ages between one million BC and 10,000 BC. Ice and snow covered much of the Yorkshire Dales, although the centre of the English ice-sheet was over the Lakeland fells. Glaciers followed the line of existing valleys scouring the landscape and taking soil and rock along with it. Glaciated U-shaped valleys were formed with steep sides and flat valley floors, as opposed to the V-shape of natural river valleys. Soil and less resistant rock were stripped from the hills leaving exposed limestone rock strata, which can be seen today in the form of limestone pavements and scars. At Kilnsey the outcrop of Great Scar Limestone was undercut by glacial erosion leaving an overhanging rock face. As the glaciers retreated with the warming of the climate, soil and rock were dropped. This can be seen in the form of moraines which are crescent shaped ridges of glacial boulder clay across the valley floor deposited by a melting glacier. Moraines often trapped meltwater forming small lakes, examples of which are Semerwater and Malham Tarn. Most of these glacial lakes have gone but their former sites are often the first to flood during rainy weather. The road between Grinton and Fremington in Swaledale follows the line of a moraine across the valley. Drumlins occur in the lower reaches of the Dales most frequently in Craven and Ribblesdale, and are small rounded 'egg shaped' mounds or hills of glacial boulder clay caused by retreating glaciers, examples of which can also be seen in mid-Wensleydale around Bainbridge. Often huge pieces of rock weighing several tons were transported many miles by the glaciers; these are known as glacial erratics, examples of which are the Norber Erratics near Austwick which are large boulders of Silurian slate resting on a limestone plateau, as well as the Carlow Stone beside Semerwater. The meltwaters were responsible for the many dry valleys and gorges which can be found in the limestone country. These were formed by water flowing over frozen ground eroding away rocks and soil thus creating valleys, however, as the climate warmed the water went underground leaving the valleys dry. Most spectacular of all would have been the waterfall over Malham Cove; with a drop of over 70 metres this would have dwarfed Niagara Falls!

FAUNA AND FLORA

Due to the varied geology, geography and climate of the Yorkshire Dales there is an enormous diversity and abundance of plants, flowers, birds, insects and animals.

The soils which cover the underlying rock strata are directly formed from these rocks. Limestone areas are characterised by thin, well drained, calcium rich soils which support an abundant and diverse plant life. Grassland dominates the scene characterised by springy, bright green turf. Some of the original open woodland can still be found across this limestone landscape, including the extensive ancient woodland of Grass Wood near Grassington, home to many species of flowering plants as well as native tree species. Ancient woodland can also be found along the limestone scars on the steep valley sides, with ash, willow, birch and hazel dominating. The many sheltered crevices in the limestone rock support numerous rare plants including green speenwort, purple wild thyme, salad burnet, herb paris, angular soloman's seal and dog's mercury.

The soils that overlie the sandstones are gritty and low in nutrients whilst shales produce soils heavy in clay. Upland areas with underlying sandstone or gritstone rocks lack calcium which assists with the decomposition of plant material, therefore there is a build up of decaying plant matter which in turn impedes drainage of this otherwise porous rock. This process has been on-going for over 7,000 years and has created a water-logged, anaerobic and acidic peat layer up to four metres thick, which supports only a handful of plant species notably cotton-grass and sphagnum moss (the key ingredient of peat formation), as well as bog asphodel, common butterwort grass and the rare insect-eating sundew. Heather (common ling, cross-leaved and bell), bracken and bilberry flourish where there is better drainage – this is often man-made to provide heather for grouse moors. The peat and heather moors are fragile and prone to erosion due to pollution, over-grazing and too many boots. This open moorland is of international importance for ground-nesting birds such as curlew, lapwing, golden plover and the ubiquitous red grouse. In fact, the heather moors are managed for the benefit of the grouse by rotational burning that creates a patchwork of young shoots and older plants for the grouse to feed on and nest in. This ensures that enough red grouse are reared for the Glorious Twelfth of August when the grouse shooting season begins.

It is where limestone, gritstone and shale are found together that the most varied flora can be seen, and Wensleydale is one of the finest areas in the country for variety of plants. The soils of the valley floor are richer, mainly due to glacial deposits, and support hay meadows. Deciduous woodland, predominantly oak, can be found in the lower reaches of the Dales.

The uplands are home to birds such as curlews, short-eared owls, oystercatchers, skylarks, kestrels, merlins and buzzards as well as both red and the much rarer black grouse. The fields and meadows of the valleys attract meadow pipits, house martins, swallows, pied and yellow wagtails. Along the riverbank you may spot herons, dippers, kingfishers, sandmartins or sandpipers. Woodpeckers, dunnocks, pheasant and nuthatches can be seen in woodland areas. The Yorkshire Dales are home to a wide variety of wild mammals including rabbits, stoats, weasels, voles, hedgehogs, deer, grey and red squirrels, otters and hares. On south-facing slopes you may catch a glimpse of an adder, Britain's only poisonous snake, slow-worm or common lizard.

STAGE ONE

GRASSINGTON
to
BUCKDEN

✦

"Oh, how can I put into words the joys of a walk over country such as this; the scenes that delight the eyes, the blessed peace of mind, the sheer exuberance which fills your soul as you tread the firm turf? This is something to be lived, not read about. On these breezy heights, a transformation is wondrously wrought within you. Your thoughts are simple, in tune with your surroundings; the complicated problems you brought with you from the town are soothed away. Up here, you are near to your Creator; you are conscious of the infinite; you gain new perspectives; thoughts run in new strange channels; there are stirrings in your soul which are quite beyond the power of my pen to describe. Something happens to you in the silent places which never could in the towns, and it is a good thing to sit awhile in a quiet spot and meditate. The hills have a power to soothe and heal which is their very own. No man has ever sat alone on the top of a hill and planned a murder or a robbery, and no man ever came down from the hills without feeling in some way refreshed, and the better for his experience."

A. Wainwright,
'A Pennine Journey - The Story of a Long Walk in 1938'.

WALK INFORMATION

. . . .

Points of interest: Iron Age settlements, two nature reserves, monastic granges and roads, breathtaking limestone scenery, Norse and Anglian settlements, hunting forests, superlative views from Birks Fell and some beautiful old pubs.

Distance:

Grassington to Arncliffe	7 miles
Arncliffe to Buckden	6 miles
Total	13 miles

Time: Allow 7 hours

Terrain: The majority of this walk follows paths across rough grassy pastures, enclosed meadowland or along riverbanks. The limestone bedrock means that the ground is predominately dry and firm for most of the way. The traverse of the limestone ravine of Dib Beck is quite steep in places. There is a section of road-walking beneath Kilnsey Crag and then along a quiet country lane heading up into Littondale. The riverside path through Littondale alongside the River Skirfare between Hawkswick and Litton is rough underfoot in places and some sections of riverbank are eroding. The climb from Litton over to Buckden is long and strenuous as it heads over the exposed moorland ridge of Birks Fell. The broad summit ridge is boggy underfoot, although sections of path have been laid with flagstones.

The traverse of Dib Beck is quite steep, and there are steep drops to the side of the path across its upper slopes. The section from Litton to Buckden heads across high, remote moorland with rough boggy ground and steep sections; navigation may be difficult in poor weather. Take care walking along the road

beneath Kilnsey Crag and also through Littondale.
Limestone is slippery when wet.

Ascents:	Birks Fell:	607 metres
Viewpoints:	Descent from Lea Green towards Conistone with views towards Kilnsey Crag.	

Riverside scenery throughout Littondale. The climb over Old Cote Moor and Birks Fell offers excellent views across upper Littondale towards Pen-y-ghent whilst the descent affords superb views of Buckden Pike and Upper Wharfedale.

FACILITIES
. . . .

Grassington	Inn / B&B / Shop / P.O. / Café / Bus / Phone / Toilets / Info.
Conistone	Phone
Kilnsey	Inn / Café / Bus
Hawkswick	B&B / Camp
Arncliffe	Inn / B&B / Phone
Litton	Inn / B&B / P.O. / Phone
Buckden	Inn / B&B / Shop / Café / Bus / Phone / Toilets / Info.

ROUTE DESCRIPTION
. . . .

(Map One)

From Grassington's cobbled Market Square, walk up the Main Street to reach the Town Hall (The Devonshire Institute) where you turn left along Chapel Street. Head straight on along this road then, as you reach Town Head, turn right up along Bank Lane (SP 'Dales Way, Kettlewell, Bycliffe Road, Grass Wood Lane, Moor Lane') and follow this walled lane up out of the village. Continue on along this lane then, at the junction of tracks, turn left through a wall-gate (SP

'Dales Way, Kettlewell, Grass Wood Lane'), over a small FB across a stream and head straight on across the field, over a wall-stile then head left through a small wall-gate to join a rough track. Turn right along this rough track (SP 'Dales Way, Kettlewell') and follow the clear path straight on across undulating fields through three narrow wall gaps. After the third narrow wall gap/stile (SP 'Dales Way, Kettlewell') the path opens out onto open grassy/limestone moorland (with limestone pavements and Grass Wood across to your left) – head straight on along the wide grassy track (ignore the grassy path that branches almost immediately off to the left towards Grass Wood) to quickly join another grassy track coming in from your right, which you follow to the left then, after a few paces, you come to a fork in this grassy track. Follow the left-hand branch of this grassy track that heads along the top of a low grassy/limestone ridge (do not head down to Grass Wood). Follow this clear grassy track straight on along the top of this low grassy ridge for about 0.5 miles keeping Grass Wood and the limestone pavement to your left then, where the grassy path divides, bear left along a clear path heading across limestone pavements, then drop down for a further 0.25 miles to cross the stone wall on your left by way of a ladder-stile next to a gate at the end of the woods (SD 993 661).

Turn right immediately after the ladder-stile and follow the path that heads steeply down into a dry limestone ravine (Dib Beck) and up the other side to a wall-stile *(take care)*. After the wall-stile turn left (SP) along the clear path alongside a low stone wall on your left (ravine of Dib Beck down to your left) then, where this wall ends, carry straight across the steep slopes of the ravine then, after a while, the path heads up to the right away from the ravine (waymarkers) to reach a gate in a stone wall. The path now becomes a clear grassy track that leads straight on through a series of gates all the way down to Conistone. Turn right along the road through the village, bearing left (road sign 'Kilnsey') at the junction and large maypole in the centre of Conistone and follow this road out of the village down to reach Conistone Bridge across the River Wharfe. Immediately after the bridge take the FP on the right (SP 'Scar Laithe'). Head straight on across the field to join a wall on your left then, where this wall bends away to the left after a short distance, bear to the left across the flat field (SP) to reach the road through a gate to the right of a barn directly below Kilnsey Crag.

(Map Two)

Turn right along the road *(take care – walk in single file)* passing below Kilnsey Crag and continue along the road for a further 0.5 miles then, where the road bends to the right down towards Skirfare Bridge across the River Skirfare, take the turning to the left towards 'Arncliffe, Litton'. Follow the road heading up into Littondale passing a narrow plantation on your right after just over 0.5 miles then continue along the road for a further 0.25 miles to reach another narrow plantation and a road-bridge across Sleets Gill (small stream) just beyond the plantation. After the bridge, carry on along the road for a further 0.25 miles then, just after the foundations of a ruined barn in the field just to your right (Scar Gill Barn), take the FP to the right through a gate (SP 'Hawkswick'). Bear left down across the field to reach a gate in a fence/tumbledown wall (SP), after which continue straight on to join a track where you turn right down along the track then, as you reach the wooden house, head off the track to the left alongside the fence (passing in front of the wooden house) to reach a gate just beyond the house. Head through the gate and follow the grassy track down through another gate then straight on bearing very slightly to the right across the field to reach the road beside Hawkswick Bridge across the River Skirfare (SD 956 704).

Head right over Hawkswick Bridge then turn left and follow the road through Hawkswick then, a short distance after leaving the village, head left over a large FB over the river (SP 'Arncliffe'). Cross the bridge then turn immediately right up the ladder stile onto the riverside path (SP 'Arncliffe'). Follow the clear path along the riverbank at first then across meadows (with the river just across to your right) through a series of stiles and gates for 1.25 miles before re-joining the wooded riverbank. Follow this riverside path straight on to reach a gate beside a converted stone barn (just to the right of a large stone house) on the edge of Arncliffe (SD 934 719). Head through the gate and follow the driveway straight on to join the road beside Arncliffe church, where you turn left along the road to reach the village green. Head to the right across the green and out of the bottom right-hand corner of the village along the road towards Malham to soon reach a bridge across Cowside Beck. Cross the bridge, immediately after which (where the road bends sharp left) take the stony track straight ahead (SP 'Litton, Halton Gill').

(Map Three)

Follow this walled stony track straight on for 0.25 miles until you reach a ladder stile beside a gate at the end of the track. Cross the stile and head straight on, keeping close to the wall on your left, to reach a wall-stile in the corner of the field, after which a clear path heads straight on across pastures to reach the Nature Reserve of Scoska Wood. A well-marked riverside path (the limestone riverbed is usually dry) leads through the Nature Reserve to reach a small wall-gate at the end of the Nature Reserve, after which turn immediately left through a bridle-gate then right and follow the clear grassy path straight on across fields to reach a gate that brings you once more alongside the dry riverbed. Follow the riverside path straight on then, at the end of the riverside path, turn left through a wall-gate then turn right across the field to join a wall-corner. Carry straight on alongside the wall on your right then, as you approach the house at the end of this field, head right through a gate on to reach a stony track opposite a ruined barn (SD 905 739). Turn right along the track, over a large ford across the Skirfare then follow the track to the left alongside the dry riverbed then, where the track forks, follow the right-hand walled track up to join the road at Litton. *(If ford impassable – as you join the stony track opposite the ruined barn, turn left then immediately right after the barn over a small bridge across a stream after which turn right down alongside the stream then bear left across fields to reach a FB across the river, after which head straight up between the houses to join the road in the centre of Litton. Turn right to reach the Queen's Arms).*

Turn right along the road passing in front of the Queen's Arms immediately after which take the lane to the left (SP 'Buckden') passing to the right of the pub and follow this up through a farmyard then continue straight on up along the walled stony track to reach a gate, after which continue on along the grassy track down to a FB across Crystal Beck. Cross the FB and through the gate ahead, after which head straight on up the steep grassy hillside alongside the wall on your right to reach a gate. Head through the gate and continue straight on along the clear stony path climbing steeply up alongside the wall (above Smearbeck Wood) then, after a short distance, the stony path slants steeply up the hillside (leaving the wall behind) to reach another gate in a wall. Head through this gate and continue up along the clear stony path slanting up across the steep hillside then through a large wall gap (no gate), after which follow the grassy path as it swings sharply round to the left to join the stone wall on your left which you follow straight up the hillside for 0.3 miles to reach a bridle-gate in a wall across your path (limestone changes to gritstone beneath your feet). Head through this bridle-gate and continue straight on for a further 0.5 miles alongside the wall climbing more steeply up across some low gritstone outcrops, above which the path begins to level out and leads up (still with the wall on your left) across the wide summit ridge (stone-flagged path) to reach a gate in a wall corner across your path on the summit of Birks Fell (SD 925 749). *(Trig Point 200 yards to the right marks Firth Fell (207m); Birks Fell summit (610m) lies 1 mile to NW. This broad moorland ridge is commonly known as Birks Fell).*

Head through the gate and continue straight on alongside the wall (stone-flagged path) then, after about 100 yards where the wall curves away to the left, continue straight on along the path (flagged at first then a wide rough path) to soon join a tumbledown wall on your left. Follow this tumbledown wall gently dropping down the hillside then, as the wall gently curves to the right after about 100 yards, turn left through a clear wall-gap. After the wall-gap, follow the clear stony path to the right to quickly reach the brow of the hillside (large cairn), where Buckden comes into view ahead far below. Follow the clear stony path bearing slightly to the left heading quite steeply down across the hillside, then down along a stone-flagged section of path. At the bottom of the flagstones, continue quite steeply down along the clear path (heading towards Buckden) then, as you reach the bottom of the steep hillside (where the hillside levels out slightly onto a wide 'shelf' of land), follow the clear path bearing to the left down across the gently sloping shelf of land (blue waymarker posts) for approx. 0.5 miles to reach a clear, stony track across your path (with a ruinous barn just to your left and the woodland of Water Gill Wood ahead). Turn left along this stony track (SP) down to reach a gate that leads through some sheep pens, after which follow the stony track winding down across the hillside, passing Redmire Farm across to your right, to join the road (SD 936 775). Turn right along the road, over the bridge across the River Wharfe and up into Buckden.

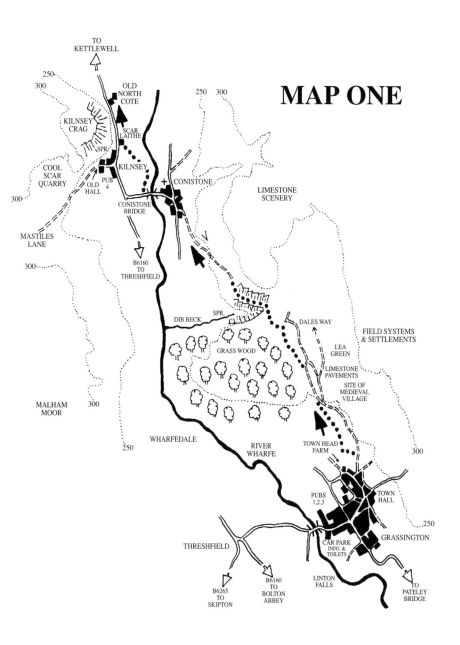

MAP ONE

TO KETTLEWELL

250
300

OLD NORTH COTE

250   300

KILNSEY CRAG

SCAR LAITHE

SPR.

COOL SCAR QUARRY

KILNSEY

PUB 4

OLD HALL

CONISTONE

300

CONISTONE BRIDGE

MASTILES LANE

300

B6160 TO THRESHFIELD

LIMESTONE SCENERY

SPR.

DIB BECK   SPR.

DALES WAY

GRASS WOOD

LEA GREEN

FIELD SYSTEMS & SETTLEMENTS

LIMESTONE PAVEMENTS

SITE OF MEDIEVAL VILLAGE

MALHAM MOOR

300

WHARFEDALE

250

RIVER WHARFE

TOWN HEAD FARM

300

PUBS 1,2,3

TOWN HALL

.250

THRESHFIELD

CAR PARK INFO. & TOILETS

GRASSINGTON

LINTON FALLS

B6265 TO SKIPTON

B6160 TO BOLTON ABBEY

TO PATELEY BRIDGE

©Crown Copyright 2005. All rights reserved. Licence Number 100011978

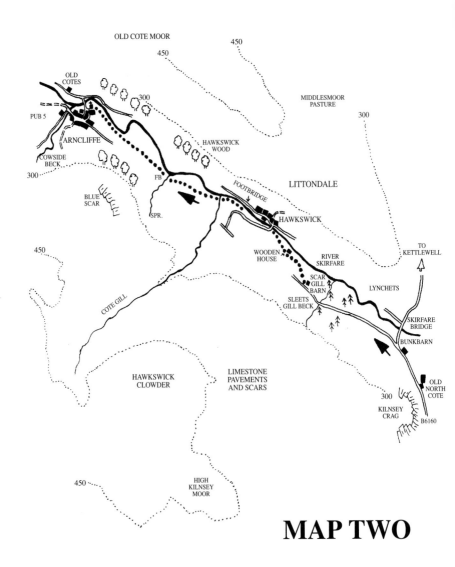

MAP TWO

©Crown Copyright 2005. All rights reserved. Licence Number 100011978

MAP THREE

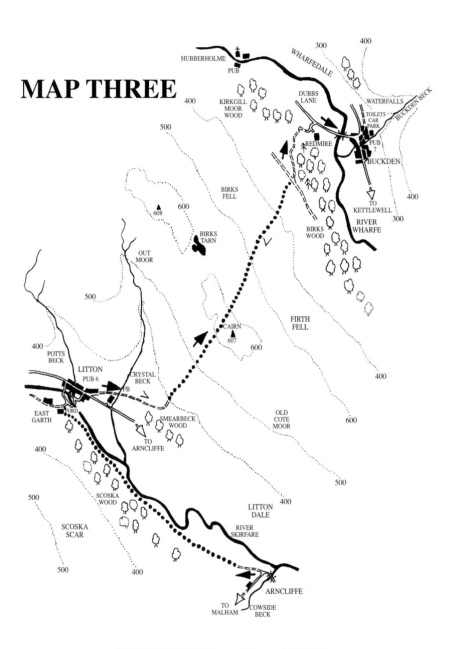

HUBBERHOLME

PUB

WHARFEDALE

300

400

DUBBS LANE

KIRKGILL MOOR WOOD

400

WATERFALLS

BUCKDEN BECK

TOILETS CAR PARK

500

REDMIRE

PUB 7

BUCKDEN

BIRKS FELL

608

600

BIRKS TARN

BIRKS WOOD

TO KETTLEWELL

300

400

RIVER WHARFE

OUT MOOR

500

FIRTH FELL

CAIRN

607

600

400

POTTS BECK

LITTON

PUB 6

CRYSTAL BECK

400

FB

EAST GARTH

FORD

SMEARBECK WOOD

OLD COTE MOOR

600

400

TO ARNCLIFFE

400

500

SCOSKA WOOD

LITTON DALE

400

SCOSKA SCAR

RIVER SKIRFARE

500

500

400

600

ARNCLIFFE

TO MALHAM

COWSIDE BECK

©Crown Copyright 2005. All rights reserved. Licence Number 100011978

GRASSINGTON, pronounced 'Girston' locally, is an attractive small town set in the heart of Wharfedale, a popular tourist destination due to its picturesque cobbled square, stone cottages and winding alleyways that beckon you to explore. People have been living in this area for over 2,000 years, originally at Lea Green and since Norman times at Grassington. The Domesday Book of 1086 estimated the number of families living in the area to be twelve. After the Norman Conquest the manorial ownership passed from the powerful de Percy family of Northumberland to the Plumptons, then to the Cliffords of Skipton Castle and finally, in the mid 18th Century, to the Dukes of Devonshire. In the late 13th Century Robert de Plumpton built the Old Hall as his hunting lodge; the building survives today as one of the oldest inhabited houses in England, despite much modification in the 16th and 17th Centuries. The Plumptons were Lords of the Manor until the 16th Century and had links with the monks of Fountains Abbey; indeed one reason for Grassington's growth was that it lay at the crossroads of two ancient roads, the monastic route from Fountains Abbey to their grazing areas above Kilnsey, and the road from Skipton to Richmond. The monks had a farm at Grassington known as Hardy Grange, which can still be found hidden away along Gills Fold although the present building is largely 17th Century. It is believed that there is an underground passage which runs from the Old Hall to Hardy Grange. Grassington was granted a market charter in 1282, thus ensuring a rise in its importance within the local rural economy and the village soon developed as a trading centre in the Forest of Wharfedale; these weekly markets continued until the late 19th Century.

The real boom period for Grassington was during the 18th and 19th Centuries when the Duke of Devonshire developed the lead mines at Yarnbury on the moors above Grassington. Many mining families moved to the area from Cornwall and Derbyshire and population levels were similar to those we see today. However, cheaper imports and dwindling reserves meant that by the end of the 19th Century mining had come to an end. *"Although Grassington suffered greatly from the stoppage of the lead mines, it is now fast becoming popular as a health resort, and, as a native female quaintly remarked, 'We've gotten t' tellygraf; all 'at we're shot on nah is t' raelwey, an' then 'appen we'd keep ahr men at hoam."* (**E. Bogg 'A Thousand Miles in Wharfedale' 1892**). The railway came to Grassington in 1902 when a branch line was built from Skipton to Threshfield, just across the River Wharfe from Grassington. This line was known as the Yorkshire Dales Railway and it brought new life to the area through tourism, indeed, there were plans to extend the line up through Wharfedale to link up with the Wensleydale Railway. The line was never a great success as passenger numbers were seasonal, and the line was predominantly used by freight. Passenger services ended in 1930 and Grassington Station closed entirely in 1968, although most of the line is still open for freight traffic serving the large and unsightly Swinden Quarry near Linton. *"Grassington seemed a busy, thriving place as we came down to it from the hill settlement on a July afternoon. A farmer and his dog drove a flock of lambs and newly clipped sheep up the lane to the pastures. The frenzy of the coming haytime was in the air. Barns were cleared; sledges lay ready in the farmyards; and the cobbled streets resounded to the rattle of reapers on their way to the meadows. The clang of the anvil and the smell of burning horn came from the blacksmith's shop, and a newly shod horse clattered home ready for the strenuous work for the next few weeks."* (**E. Pontefract & M. Hartley 'Wharfedale' 1938**).

Today Grassington is a popular tourist centre whose charm is not just the picturesque cobbled market square with its many interesting shops and old fashioned inns, but the hidden alleyways, known locally as folds, which lead off it. In the centre of The Square is The Pump, otherwise known as the Fountain, a recently restored water pump that supplied the town's drinking water in the 19th Century. Look out for the circular stone set into the cobbles nearby which once had a ring used to tether bulls for baiting. *"Wrinkled, winding alleys branch everywhere as the whim takes them. Pursuing these, you happen, when least expecting it, on a farmstead and the sweet breath of cattle."* (**H. Sutcliffe 'The Striding Dales' 1929**). The many folds were originally crofts running back from the main street, however over the centuries they have been in-filled with houses and miners' cottages.

Buildings of interest include 'Theatre Cottage' off Garrs Lane, which was originally a barn where a theatre was housed in the early 19th Century; Edmund Kean and Harriet Mellon appeared here in 1807. The rough lane that leads off Garrs Lane, known locally as Water Lane, is thought to follow the line of the Roman Road between Ilkley and Bainbridge. Hidden away off this lane is Pletts Barn, a wonderful example of a 17th Century stone-built barn with exquisite details including dovecotes and a cobbled forecourt where John Wesley once preached in the late 18th Century. Town Head Farm is one of the town's finest buildings and a superb example of a 17th Century Dales farmhouse with stone mullion windows and a protruding two-storey porch. This farm belongs to the Trustees of the Fountaine Hospital at Linton and provides revenue for Fountaine Hospital almshouses. Grassington Town Hall and Devonshire Institute stands at the top of Main Street, built in 1855 originally as a Mechanics Institute but given to the new Parish Council by the Duke of Devonshire in the late 19th Century. It was extended in the 1920s and again in 1998 to provide more modern facilities for theatre, festivals and exhibitions. On the main street is an old blacksmith's shop that was once owned by Tom Lee, local blacksmith and notorious robber. In 1766 Dr Richard Petty knew of Lee's mischievous ways and threatened to tell the authorities, however, after an evening at a Kilnsey hostelry, Tom Lee murdered Dr Petty on his way home through Grass Wood, and then carried his body down along the riverside path and threw it into the Wharfe at Loup Scar near Burnsall. He was only caught after his servant broke down and confessed, and Lee was sentenced to hang at York and his body gibbeted in Grass Wood; his gibbet irons are supposedly buried on the small mound near to the 17th Century Grassington Bridge across the River Wharfe.

LEA GREEN is an area of grassy moorland a mile or so to the north of Grassington, which boasts one of the largest Iron Age settlements in England that was occupied from 200BC until 400AD, surviving throughout the Roman occupation because of its secluded location high on the hills. Rectangular fields, hut circles and traces of roads can be clearly seen, although to the untrained eye it appears to be a very rough scattering of fields covered with lots of grassy bumps! As with many other archaeological sites, the true picture only really comes to life when viewed from the air, although its windswept location certainly stirs the imagination. *"The antiquity of this district is best proved by its earthworks and the remains of early Celtic days, which are to be seen just on the outskirts of the village to the north-west. These carry the mind back to a period when Druidical superstition prevailed in the forest, and the Roman eagle waved on the moorland."* (E. Bogg 1892).

The footpath between Grassington and Dib Beck skirts the southern and western edge of the Lea Green Iron Age site, however, the footpath does cross the site of the medieval village of Grassington, with more defined and regular grass-covered earthworks and bumps in the fields between Town Head Farm and Grass Wood. This was the site of the original village of Grassington, which was established by Anglo-Saxon settlers in the 7th Century but abandoned in the 12th Century when the Manor was transferred from the Percys of Northumberland to the Plumpton family and the present-day town established just to the south. Indeed, the name of the town is thought to be derived from a Saxon farmer called Garr who settled in this area and cleared an enclosure or 'tun'.

GRASS WOOD is a beautiful swathe of ancient semi-natural woodland that covers around 260 acres and once formed part of the much larger Forest of Wharfedale. *"The Wharfe loves these woods and makes itself especially beautiful for them. A path on the right bank takes one through the meadows over stiles, then past quiet pools, rushes, falls and the Ghaistrills or spirit-holes, where the river hurrying into a narrow passage concentrates its full force till, set free, it rushes madly foaming into the next reach."* (C. Lewis 'Wharfedale'). It is a fascinating place with many native tree species including oak, ash, hazel and birch as well as over 70 varieties of flowering plants that thrive in the calcareous soils beneath the tree canopy, including bluebell, dog's mercury, orchids, wild thyme, marjoram, basil, stone bramble, mountain melick, melancholy thistle, betony and the extremely rare rock whitebeam. It also boasts many archaeological remains thus meriting Nature Reserve and Site of Special Scientific Interest protection. It is a wonderful place to explore in spring when the woods come alive with birdsong and wild flowers. *"When you have known it a little time you have a personal feeling for the wood. It is alive, and entering it you feel welcomed or repelled as you would on meeting a person."* (**E. Pontefract & M. Hartley 1938**). Hidden away amongst the trees are the impressive stone ramparts and ditches of an ancient British hill-fort known as Fort Gregory that was built by the Brigantes tribes in around AD70, as well as the well-preserved remains of a small Iron Age settlement.

Just to the north of Grass Wood, our route crosses the impressive limestone ravine of Dib Beck. This steep-sided wooded ravine was scoured out by glacial meltwaters towards the end of the last Ice Age when the permafrost prevented the water from seeping down through the limestone bed-rock. This whole area boasts some wonderful limestone scenery with pavements, dry valleys and outcrops all around. From Dib Beck, a track leads down to Conistone with superb views towards the impressive bulk of Kilnsey Crag.

CONISTONE is a fine example of an Anglian settlement that can trace its origins back to the 8th Century, with meadowland by the river, ploughing terraces on the hillside slopes, common land on the fells and houses grouped around a green complete with maypole. These ploughing terraces, known as lynchets, are flat terraces cut into the hillside wide enough for oxen to pull a plough; these terraces allowed crops to be grown on the otherwise steep valley sides. The lynchets surrounding Conistone most probably date back to those early Anglo-Saxon farmers who settled in this area, although most date from the medieval period. The presence of these terraces indicates that the climate in the Yorkshire Dales several centuries ago was much warmer than today, which allowed farmers to grow crops.

St Mary's Church is the oldest church in the southern Yorkshire Dales that dates back to pre-Conquest times. It still has some pre-Norman arches as well as wealth of other interesting features including a poor box and Norman font, despite extensive 'restoration' in 1846. *"If we could lift the curtain which hides the past, many a stirring scene and gathering of bygone people, peasant and monk, should we witness in and around this old kirkyard – the smile and gladness of a bridal party leaving the holy fane, or sounds of merrymaking greeting the ear – many a sign of tragedy throwing its shadow of human passion and errance on the mind-picture."* (**E. Bogg 'By the Banks of the Wharfe' 1921**). In the graveyard is a sad memorial to a group of six young men who were killed by rising floodwaters whilst they were exploring nearby Mossdale Caverns on the 24th June 1967, in what was (and still is) England's worst caving accident. This is a notoriously difficult cave system with a labyrinth of narrow passageways that were sealed up after the tragedy, leaving the young men in their final resting place within the cave.

Conistone is a beautiful but sleepy village with lovely old stone cottages and farms that seem to blend in perfectly with the surrounding limestone hills. Unfortunately there is no pub, *"...you can call for a cup of tea and a rest at the Post Office or at Mrs. Hill's, but remember nothing 'stronger' can be got in the way of liquid refreshment, as Conistone and Thorpe are the only villages in Upper Wharfedale without an inn."* (**J. Crowther 'Rambles Round Grassington' 1920**).

KILNSEY is dominated by its impressive crag; *"It is a natural phenomenon which reduces everything near it into insignificance. Its huge bulk jutting like a clenched fist into the valley dominates the middle dale."* (**E. Pontefract & M. Hartley 1938**). The crag is 170-feet high with an overhang of 40-feet that was undercut by the scouring action of glaciers thousands of years ago to create this classic example of a truncated spur. This overhanging rock face now poses a challenge to climbers, *"...overhangs road and river as if threatening to crush whatever passes. Around this frowning rock all sorts of legends and fairy tales centre, and the village at its foot was once the abode of two witches who practised divination and sold charms."* (**Fletcher 'Nooks and Corners of Yorkshire'**). Clear, cool springs bubble up from the foot of the crag and it is said to be impossible to hit the crag with a stone thrown from the road. Behind the Crag is the huge and unsightly Cool Scar Quarry. What madness allows a quarry here? The stone will be used for motorways, or gardens, or paths so that more people can be whisked here in greater numbers in the luxury of their cars and meanwhile more and more of what they have come to see will be torn away to provide quicker access to see it.

The village of Kilnsey developed as a grange for Fountains Abbey in the 12th Century, as the Abbey owned vast areas of grazing lands on the moors above Kilnsey. Mastiles Lane was originally a monastic drovers' road which connected Fountains Abbey with grazing lands throughout the Yorkshire Dales and as far as Borrowdale in the Lake District; today it is a superb green lane. *"It (Kilnsey) has an ancient appearance, and only consists of some twelve houses, two of which are the 'Tenants Arms and the Anglers' Inn."* (**J. Crowther 1920**). The Anglers Arms, now closed, was where Dr Petty spent his last night before being murdered by Tom Lee in Grass Woods, a crime for which he was later hanged. Dr Petty's horse is said to haunt the woods. Behind the remaining inn stands the magnificent Kilnsey Old Hall which was built in 1648 on the site of the grange; Lady Anne Clifford used to stay at the Old Hall on her travels. The Hall had been neglected for many years and was used as a barn, however, it has recently been restored to its former glory; all that remains of the grange is part of the gatehouse.

LITTONDALE, originally known as Amerdale, is the main tributary of the River Wharfe in Upper Wharfedale and is a classic example of a glaciated U-shaped valley with flat valley pastures and steep wooded sides. The valley is drained by the delightful River Skirfare, which means 'bright stream' in Old Norse. This river is born on the eastern flanks of Pen-y-ghent (694 metres) and Plover Hill where three streams – Pen-y-ghent Gill, Foxup Beck and Cosh Beck – tumble down from the moorland heights to form the Skirfare. This valley is one of the most beautiful in England and is also noted for its variety of rare plants and flowers; the steep valley sides and limestone scars provide the ideal safe habitat for such flora. *"Littondale is a pageant of loveliness all along its length and attains near perfection at Arncliffe."* (**A. Wainwright 'In the Limestone Dales' 1991**). Littondale is also steeped in history. There are traces of Iron Age settlements on the moors and the villages of today originally started life as Anglian settlements or Norse farmsteads in pre-Conquest times. After the Norman Conquest, Littondale was a hunting forest, then the Cistercian monks of Fountains Abbey used the limestone pastures for grazing their vast flocks of sheep as they once owned over 100 square miles of land centred on Malham, Littondale and Wharfedale – a quick glance at the map will reveal many reminders of this once powerful monastic landowner with names such as Monk's Road, Fountains Fell and many more still in use today. The Dissolution of the Monasteries may have changed land ownership but did little to alter either land use or the way of life which, coupled with the fact that Littondale is one of the few valleys to have escaped the ravages of mining or quarrying, means that the landscape and villages remain well preserved. Littondale has many literary connections; Wordsworth mentioned it in his poem 'The White Doe of Rylstone', Charles Kingsley wrote about it in 'The Water Babies' and it was often used for locations in the television series Emmerdale Farm between 1972 and 1976, its name derived from 'Amerdale'.

HAWKSWICK, is named after the birds of prey that once soared from the surrounding scars and crags. It is a tiny farming hamlet, with beautiful old limestone farmhouses and wonderful views across the dale. *"In Hawkswick itself there is scarcely room by the river for houses; barn doors open towards the water's edge and one can sit and watch ducks from the breakfast table."* (**N. Duerden 'Portrait of the Dales' 1978**). The footpath alongside the River Skirfare between Hawkswick and Arncliffe is an absolute delight with river, meadows and steep valley sides creating a near-perfect scene.

ARNCLIFFE was originally an Anglian settlement whose original medieval layout has survived intact: a large village green around which houses huddle with crofts running back from the village. It is this combination of old stone houses and barns overlooking the spacious village green with the steep valley slopes sweeping up to the wild moors that give this village such a timeless beauty. The name means 'eagle cliff'; the scars above Arncliffe would have been ideal nesting sites for birds of prey. The village is situated beside the confluence of Cowside Beck and the Skirfare, set amongst trees and sheltered by steep valley slopes. Cowside Beck cuts a deep ravine just to the south-west of the village, its gleaming white limestone scars rising sheer from the narrow valley floor. Above these scars a narrow path, known as Monk's Road, leads from Arncliffe high above Cowside Beck before heading across remote moorland to join Mastiles Lane near Malham Tarn. This old road would have been used by the monks of Fountains Abbey in medieval times to reach their farms and grazing lands in Littondale.

There has been a church at Arncliffe most probably since Saxon times, although it was not until the early 12th Century that a church was built in stone, which was in turn replaced by a new church in Tudor times built on the foundations of this Norman church. The present church, dedicated to St Oswald, dates mainly from 1796 and 1841 when the Tudor building was pulled down and 'restoration' took place. The church tower survived and dates back to the late 15th Century. Inside the church there is a memorial to the local men who fought at the Battle of Flodden Field in 1513. This battle was one of the most famous and bloodiest fought during the Border Troubles between Scotland and England that took place near Wooler in Northumberland. It resulted in the death of James IV of Scotland, most of his nobles and 10,000 Scottish soldiers at the hands of the English army under the command of the Earl of Surrey; James IV was the last British monarch to die in battle. The church also has one of the oldest bells in the country, dated 1350, which was probably a gift from Fountains Abbey. *"The little river (Skirfare) is one of Yorkshire's most enchanting streams, and Arncliffe has an exquisite share of its valley, the village deep-set like a jewel between the wooded slopes of the moors and fells. The houses are round a green, and the Cowside Beck falls into the stream before it flows under a beautiful bow bridge and cascades by the churchyard. It would be hard to imagine a lovelier setting for the church, a simple place with a grey medieval tower peeping over a mantle of trees."* **(A. Mee 'Yorkshire West Riding' 1941).** It is a place of peace and tranquillity where ancient stones, mature trees and flowing river combine; a place to pause and gather your thoughts.

The Falcon Inn is a superb example of a traditional Dales pub with wooden settles, open fires and beer straight from the cask, a living and integral part of our culture and heritage that has been run by the same family for four generations. *"The Falcon Inn stands as such a tavern should, unobtrusive in its simple dignity, instinct with the hospitality of other days."* (H. Sutcliffe 1929). There are some beautiful old stone barns which face onto the green; these barns were built at a time when crops were grown in the dale and were therefore designed with a porched doorway which allowed carts to be brought in under shelter, and rear doors which created a draft for threshing. Between Arncliffe and Litton lies Scoska Wood which is the largest ash and rowan wood left in the Yorkshire Dales, now protected as a nature reserve. The River Skirfare is also at its most playful in this area with the water disappearing beneath its bed of huge shelves of limestone rock, only reappearing again after heavy rain.

LITTON grew around the busy fording point where the old packhorse route from Wharfedale crossed the River Skirfare before climbing across the flanks of Fountains Fell by way of an old 'green' lane across Dawson Close over the hills to Ribblesdale and Settle. The monks of Fountains Abbey had a hospice here too. It is a village of attractive houses, farms and barns strung out along a narrow lane with the unspoilt Queens Arms Inn at one end and a small 'green' at the other. This whitewashed inn has been refreshing travellers passing its door for over 160 years, although it probably provided refreshments as far back as the 18th Century; I recommend you do the same before the arduous climb over Birks Fell to Buckden. It is a classic example of an old Dales drovers' inn with flagstone floors, low beams and a roaring fire, and is also the home of Litton Ale Brewery. *"The Buckden track joins the road by the house which has been an inn since 1842. The original inn, down a grassy lane between the road and the river, is now a barn....It was last kept by an old woman called Mrs Taylor. She avoided paying for a licence by selling penny or halfpenny parkins, and giving beer or ale with them. Now cows munch hay where her patrons ate parkin and drank 'free' beer."* (E. Pontefract & M. Hartley 1938).

BIRKS FELL, at 610 metres or 2,001-ft, only just qualifies for mountain status (a hill above two thousand feet). On old imperial maps the highest point was shown as 2001-ft, but this was revised to 608 metres upon metric conversion, which is just below the magic 2,000-ft required for a mountain. But walkers knew different, and in 2006 Ordnance Survey agreed that Birks Fell was, indeed, one foot above two thousand feet; the new 610 metre spot height lies just to the north-west of Birks Tarn. It is more fell than mountain in character with boggy terrain and windswept moorland. Birks Fell actually forms part of a high moorland ridge that runs for several miles between Upper Wharfedale and Littondale, with numerous named fell tops that are little more than undulations along the ridge, including Horse Head, Firth Fell and Old Cote Moor Top. Rarely dipping below 600 metres, this broad ridge is criss-crossed by several inter-valley bridleways and footpaths that date back to the packhorse days. The view from the top of Birks Fell, between Litton and Buckden, is breathtaking, with fine views towards Buckden cradled beneath the towering heights of Buckden Pike. The name of this moorland mountain is derived from the Old Norse words meaning 'birch hill', for its lower slopes are still cloaked with ancient woodland. *"The outlook over Kettlewelldale from the edge of the moor at this spot is magnificent indeed; the rich green valley, with its river wandering dreamily, the villages reposing as in a charmed sleep in the embrasures of the eternal hills; and all the accessories of colour, light and shadow which are required to make a striking picture are found here."* (**E. Bogg 1921**).

BUCKDEN is the first, or last, village in Wharfedale and so has an air of importance about it. The wild valley of Langstrothdale, as the upper reaches of the River Wharfe are known, cuts a meandering 'V' through the high fells bringing the infant Wharfe down to join the waters of Cray Gill just to the north-west of Buckden – it is at this point that Wharfedale begins, a wonderful example of a U-shaped glaciated valley encircled by the looming bulks of Birks Fell, Horse Head Moor, Yockenthwaite Moor and Buckden Pike. It grew in importance in Norman times when the area between Buckden and the dale head was a hunting forest known as Langstrothdale Chase, from the Norman French word 'chasse' meaning 'hunting'. Indeed, the name of the village is derived from the Old English words meaning 'valley of the bucks'. A mile to the south of the village stands Buckden Cross, which marked the limit of the old hunting forest, the preserve of the Earls of Northumberland who had been granted the hunting rights by the King. This forest was governed by its own laws, courts and privileges, and many of the forest officials would have lived at Buckden. *"In olden time Langstrothdale was one vast forest, and, in the memory of aged inhabitants, much more densely wooded than at present; the mountain slopes on the southern side of the stream are still well wooded. The dark green of the firs and the wild-looking glens present an appearance of weird grandeur truly Alpine."* (E. Bogg 1892).

The hunting forest was of little commercial value to these Norman lords, and so over the centuries most of the land was granted to monasteries, including Coverham Abbey and particularly Fountains Abbey who owned vast swathes of land between Langstrothdale and Fountains Fell. The monks not only developed vast sheep walks, but also began to exploit the mineral wealth by mining lead as well as coal to fire the smelt mills, albeit on a small scale. The village remained a small farming community until the late 17th Century when the Earl of Burlington began to develop lead mining on the flanks of Buckden Pike; these mineral rights later passed to the Duke of Devonshire in the mid 18th Century. The Buckden Lead Mine dates back to 1697 and was in use until the late 19th Century when the mines closed due to cheaper imports. The old levels, spoil heaps and ruined smelt mill lie at the head of the deep cleft of Buckden Beck surrounded by dramatic scenery. It was during the boom years of the lead mines that the village flourished, with two autumn fairs and three inns; now all that remains is the Buck Inn.

Tourism has made more of an obvious impression at Buckden than most Dales villages, as the large car park and numerous holiday cottages testify, fortunately its setting amongst the fells can never be changed. *"...perched on the hillside like a Tibetan monastery..."* (A. Wainwright 'A Pennine Journey - The Story of a Long Walk in 1938' 1986). If you explore the many lanes that lead from the Buck Inn away from the main road you will discover the old 'heart' of Buckden with many lovely old cottages, farms, Wesleyan Chapel and village hall. *"Buckden. So cradled is it in the heights that we seem to be inside a stupendous bowl as we stand where the farms and cottages and the ivied inn are gathered by the green."* **(A. Mee 1941).** Buckden Pike, Wharfedale's second highest fell, rises behind the village to a height of 702 metres (2,302 feet). Just to the south of the summit is a memorial cross erected in memory of the five Polish crew of a RAF Wellington bomber that crashed during a snow storm in 1942. There was one survivor. Badly injured, he followed footprints in the snow of a fox, which eventually led him to the White Lion Inn at Cray and safety. A bronze head of a fox peeps out from the base of the cross, the lone survivor's personal tribute to the fox that led him to safety.

Much of Upper Wharfedale, including Heber Farm, the last working farm in Buckden, is now in the care of the National Trust who manage and protect over 6,100 acres of environmentally important and sensitive meadowland, ancient woodland and moorland stretching from Kettlewell to Beckermonds. The National Trust has converted Town Head Barn in the heart of Buckden to provide information and education about life and the landscape in Upper Wharfedale.

Top: Leaving Grassington
Middle: The Falcon, Arncliffe
Bottom: Grassington
© Mark Reid 2008

Top: Buckden
Middle: Buckden Rake
Bottom: Above Cray
© *Mark Reid 2008*

Top: Bainbridge
Middle: Askrigg
Bottom: Oxnop Scar
© Mark Reid 2008

Top: Ivelet Bridge
Middle: Reeth
Bottom: Calver Hill
© Mark Reid 2008

Top: Bolton Castle
Middle: St. Andrew's Church
Bottom: Aysgarth Falls
© *Mark Reid 2008*

Top: West Burton Falls
Middle: Horsehouse
Bottom: Hunters Stone
© Mark Reid 2008

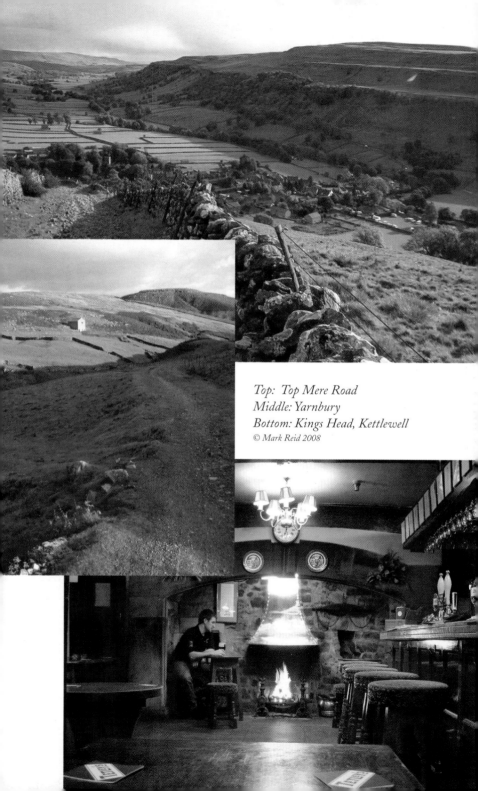

Top: Top Mere Road
Middle: Yarnbury
Bottom: Kings Head, Kettlewell
© *Mark Reid 2008*

Top: Hebden Gill
Middle: Old Guidepost near Thorpe
Bottom: Linton
© *Mark Reid 2008*

STAGE TWO

BUCKDEN
to
ASKRIGG

✦

"There is only one way to know a hill, and that is to put your feet on it and walk. Wander about leisurely if you wish, but better still, make the summit your objective and struggle up to it. Plunge into the bracken and heather, and wrestle with the thousand tentacles that would hold you back; splash through the streams that silver the hillside; scramble up the rocks and know the thrill that enslaves the mountaineer; sweat and pant, slip and tumble, and curse if you are so minded, and rest often. But get to the top. And if up there you find a gale so strong as to bowl you off your feet, or you are privileged to be in the nerve-centre of a thunderstorm, so much the better. Stay on the summit as long as you may, then come down. Don't tread circumspectively now, but run; run as if all the fiends of hell were loose at your heels. Run with giant strides, leap, jump, tumble and sprawl and roll, come down helter-skelter until you reach ground level in the valley. Wash in the stream, and bathe your wounds, and clean yourself up a bit. Then seek out a royal feed and a soft bed... if you have done all this, one of two things has happened to you. Either you will never want to see a hill again, in which case you may safely assume that the rot has settled in your soul so deeply that nothing will remove it; or you will hunger for the next opportunity, do it again and again, and keep young forever."

A. Wainwright,
'A Pennine Journey - The Story of a Long Walk in 1938'.

WALK INFORMATION

Points of interest:	Roman roads and forts, beautiful waterfalls, Wharfedale's highest inn, wild moorland landscapes, one of the finest 'green lane' walks in England, the legend of the flooded city, a forest village with its horn to guide travellers, fortified farmhouse and 'Skeldale House' as seen on TV.

Distance:

Buckden to Bainbridge	9.5 miles
Bainbridge to Askrigg	3.5 miles
Total	13 miles

Time: Allow 6 hours

Terrain: The initial climb out of Buckden is quite steep and rocky underfoot, although the track soon levels out, with wonderful views across Upper Wharfedale. A superb grassy track (Roman road) then leads across a shelf of land on the lower flanks of Buckden Pike to Cray High Bridge. After a short section of road walking, a clear stony track winds steeply up onto Stake Moss (exposed moorland) – the climb is not as difficult as it first appears as it follows a clear stony track that climbs quickly up onto the summit plateau. The track then heads across Stake Moss for 1.5 miles before a grassy path leads down into Cragdale and Stalling Busk. The remainder of this walk is along riverside paths and across meadowland, with a short section of road walking around Worton.

This walk involves a number of quite steep sections. The walk across the open moorland of Stake Moss is exposed to the elements, although the track on the ground is clear for most of the way. There are steep drops to the side of the path as you approach Bainbridge. Take care crossing the A684 at Worton – fast, busy road.

Ascents:	Stake Moss:	561 metres
Viewpoints:	Buckden Rake looking across Langstrothdale. Descent from Stake Moss towards Raydale. Views of Semerwater from the Ruined Church. View back towards Semerwater and out across Wensleydale from the path along the River Bain. Worton Scar looking across Bainbridge and its Roman fort.	

FACILITIES

....

Buckden	Inn / B&B / Shop / Café / Bus / Phone / Toilets / Info.
Cray	Inn
Stalling Busk	B&B / Café / Phone
Bainbridge	Inn / B&B / Shop / Café / Bus / Phone / Toilets
Worton	Inn / B&B / Bus / Phone
Askrigg	Inn / B&B / Shop / Café / Bus / Phone / Toilets

ROUTE DESCRIPTION

....

(Map Four)

Leave Buckden along the stony track at the top end of the car park (SP 'Buckden Pike & Cray High Bridge') and follow this clear track straight on (Buckden Rake) climbing steeply up through Rakes Wood. The track leads up for just over 0.5 miles to reach a gate across your path at the top of the climb, after which the track levels out for a short distance before gently rising up then, where the track divides, head straight on along the left-hand track (with the wall on your left) and through another gate (SP 'Cray High Bridge'). Follow the clear grassy track straight on across the flat shelf of land through a series of gates for approx. 1 mile all the way to reach the road beside Cray High Bridge *(Detour to the White Lion Inn at Cray - follow the clearly marked FP steeply down to the left half-way along this shelf of land)*. Turn right up along the road and follow it bending sharply up to the left then rising up onto the top of Kidstones Pass. Continue along the road for 0.25 miles then, as the road curves round to the right, take the clear wide stony track off to the left through a gate/cattle grid (SP 'Byway Stalling Busk'). Follow this clear enclosed stony track straight on, level at first then winding steeply up onto the flat plateau of Stake Moss – the track levels out and leads on across the top of the moorland to reach a gate across the track. Head through the gate and continue along the stony track heading across open moorland for a further mile to reach a second gate - SD 933 832 (where the track bends quite sharply to the right and becomes enclosed by high stone walls).

(Map Five)

Take the FP to the left immediately before this second gate (SP) over a ladder stile, and follow the clear wide grassy path straight on bearing slightly to the right down across the hillside, over a series of wall-stiles to reach a ruined barn after 0.5 miles. Cross the stile just behind the barn and follow the path bearing slightly to the right down across the hillside to reach a wall-stile immediately to the left of a gate in the stone wall on your right. After the wall-stile, follow the grassy path heading down across the hillside to join a small stream on your right which you follow down to reach a ford across Shaw Gate Gill just above some waterfalls. Cross the stream and follow the clear grassy path gently rising up, over a ladder stile then straight on (Cragdale down to your left) to reach a stile beside a gate that leads back onto the enclosed stony track (High Lane). Turn left along this track and follow it gently curving round to the right then, after 0.5 miles, take the enclosed track to the left (Bob Lane) and follow this down to join the road just above Stalling Busk (SD 917 858).

Turn left down into the village and follow the road bearing round to the right passing Home Farm then St Matthews Church then, as you reach the edge of the village, take the narrow path bearing down to the left ahead (SP 'Ruined Church'). Follow this down over a rough track then straight on along a stony track then, where this track bends to the left through a gate, carry straight on along the enclosed path over a small stone-slab FB down to reach a gate. After the gate, head down alongside the wooded stream on your left to reach the ruined church. At the church, turn right (SP 'Semerwater') alongside the churchyard wall and follow the clear path across the hillside, through the Nature Reserve and down skirting the shores of Semerwater then up through woodland to a wall-stile beside a barn, after which follow the clear path across fields to reach the road over a large ladder stile. Turn left along the road passing the parking area beside Semerwater on to reach Semerwater Bridge across the River Bain (SD 921 877). Take the FP to the right immediately before this bridge (SP 'Blean Lane, Bainbridge').

(Map Six)

Follow the clear riverside path straight on (River Bain on your left), through a gate after which continue on along the riverside path over a stile then on following the river as it bends round to the right on to reach a ladder stile beside a gate in a wall. Head over the ladder stile and follow the wide grassy path straight on gradually climbing up the hillside to reach a wall-stile beside another gate, after which head straight on through two more squeeze-stiles then head straight on up over the hill ahead (Bracken Hill), with the steep wooded gorge of the River Bain down to your left, to reach a wall-gate in the far top right-hand corner of the field (SP). After the wall-gap, head straight on along the wide grassy path heading down towards Bainbridge for 0.3 miles (SP) then, as you approach the stone wall (and road) to your right, head down alongside this wall/road on your right (River Bain now down to your left again) to join the main road just above Bainbridge. *(Detour to the left to the Rose & Crown in the centre of Bainbridge).* At the main road turn right to quickly reach a T-junction where you turn right towards 'Semerwater, Stalling Busk' then immediately left through a squeeze-stile in a wall (SP 'Cubeck').

Head up across the field, through a wall-gate to your left after which head up to the right across the field to reach a squeeze-stile at the top of the field, then carry on to quickly reach another squeeze-stile that leads onto the limestone ridge of Brough Scar (SD 938 897). Turn left alongside the wall across the top of this escarpment (passing

Scar Top Farm across to your right) and continue straight on along the top of the wooded escarpment (ignore paths down to the left) on to reach a small wall-gate that leads into woodland. Continue straight on along the clear path through the woodland (along the top of the escarpment) then, just before the wall-gate at the end of the woods, take the FP down to the left (SP 'Worton') that leads quite steeply down through the woods and out onto open fields at the bottom of the escarpment. Head to the right across the field, passing the end of a section of stone wall, then continue on towards the buildings of Worton passing the corner of a fence (signpost) then gradually drop down to join a wall above some large barns, which you follow down to the left to reach a gate that leads onto the main road at Worton. Turn right along the road *(take care)* then take the turning to the left after a short distance passing the 'phone box and follow this road straight on out of the village down over the road-bridge across the River Ure *(Detour to the Victoria Arms that avoids the main road - follow the road passing the 'phone box and take the second turning to the right ('Dead End' sign) then at the end of this lane head straight on along the enclosed path, at the end of which head right up across the field to reach the main road near the Victoria Arms).*

After Worton Bridge across the River Ure follow the road as it bends round to the right then, where the road bends to the left after a short distance, take the FP to the right through a squeeze-stile on this bend (SP 'Aysgarth'). Follow the riverside path straight on with the Ure on your right, over two footbridges across side-streams and on over a stile by a gate that leads onto a track beside the farm buildings of Nappa Mill. Turn left up along the lane then, at the 'Weak Bridge' and ford, take the FP directly ahead through a small wall-gate beside a gate (to the right of the bridge). After the wall-gate, follow the grassy track up to the right across the field to reach a gate in the top right-hand corner of the field, after which continue along the grassy track to join a walled track just below Nappa Hall (SD 965 907). Turn left along the stony track passing through the farmyard of Nappa Hall and up to reach the road. Turn left along the road, passing the turning for Nappa Scar, a short distance after which take the FP to the left (SP 'Askrigg'). Drop down the small limestone escarpment, then head to the right across the field gradually bearing away from the low wooded escarpment, then drop down over a wall-stile and on over Newbiggin Beck *(* see below)*. After the stream climb up the grassy bank ahead then on (passing just to the right of the telegraph pole with two sets of wires) to reach a wall-stile over the wall across your path - *this stile is not very obvious!* After this stile, follow the clear path straight on across several fields through wall-gates and over stiles to reach a road junction on the outskirts of Askrigg. Turn left along the road towards 'Worton' then, after a short distance, take the FP to the right just after the small road-bridge (SP), passing to the right of the workshops up to a small gate. After the gate, head straight on to join a wall on your right heading up over the hill then on to reach a gate on the edge of the village. After the gate, turn left then follow the lane round to the right passing in between the houses down to reach the main street in the centre of Askrigg (SD 949 911).

* If Newbiggin Beck is impassable, re-trace your steps back to the road at Nappa Scar. As you reach the road turn left along the footpath (signpost 'Newbiggin') that runs parallel to the road on your right. Follow this path straight on across fields (wall/road on your right) over ladder stiles/squeeze-stiles for 0.5 miles to re-join the road just before the Newbiggin turning. Turn left and follow this road (ignore turning to Newbiggin) down into Askrigg.

MAP FOUR

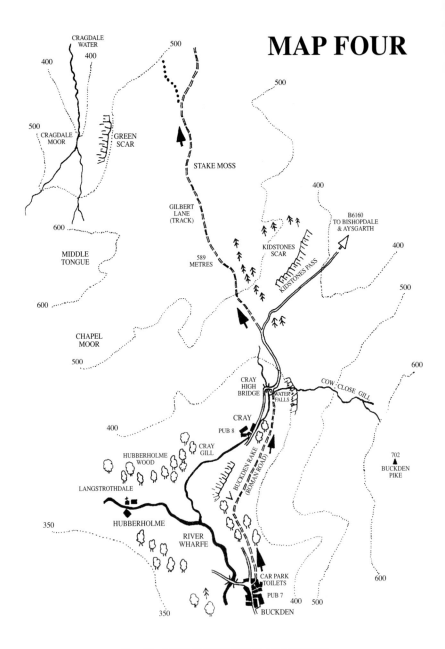

CRAGDALE
WATER

400

400

CRAGDALE
MOOR

GREEN
SCAR

500

STAKE MOSS

500

500

MIDDLE
TONGUE

600

600

GILBERT
LANE
(TRACK)

589
METRES

KIDSTONES
SCAR

KIDSTONES PASS

400

B6160
TO BISHOPDALE
& AYSGARTH

400

500

CHAPEL
MOOR

500

600

CRAY
HIGH
BRIDGE

WATER
FALLS

COW CLOSE GILL

CRAY

PUB 8

CRAY
GILL

BUCKDEN RAKE
(ROMAN ROAD)

702
BUCKDEN
PIKE

400

HUBBERHOLME
WOOD

LANGSTROTHDALE

350

HUBBERHOLME

RIVER
WHARFE

350

CAR PARK
TOILETS

PUB 7

400

500

600

BUCKDEN

©Crown Copyright 2005. All rights reserved. Licence Number 100011978

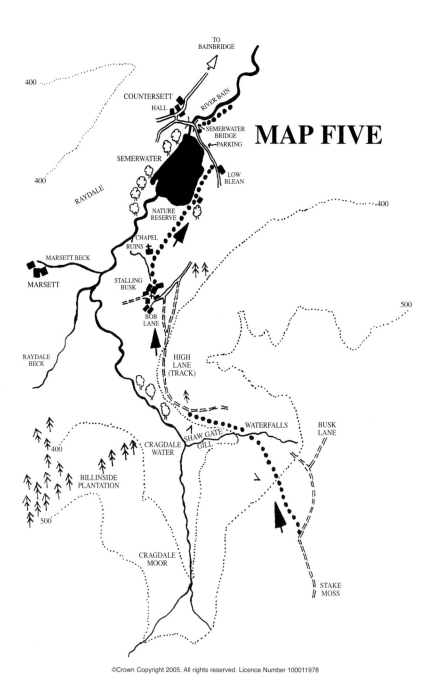

MAP FIVE

TO
BAINBRIDGE

400

COUNTERSETT
HALL

RIVER BAIN

SEMERWATER
BRIDGE
PARKING

400

SEMERWATER

RAYDALE

LOW
BLEAN

NATURE
RESERVE

CHAPEL
RUINS

MARSETT BECK

MARSETT

STALLING
BUSK

BOB
LANE

RAYDALE
BECK

HIGH
LANE
(TRACK)

500

WATERFALLS

BUSK
LANE

SHAW GATE
GILL

CRAGDALE
WATER

400

BILLINSIDE
PLANTATION

500

CRAGDALE
MOOR

STAKE
MOSS

©Crown Copyright 2005. All rights reserved. Licence Number 100011978

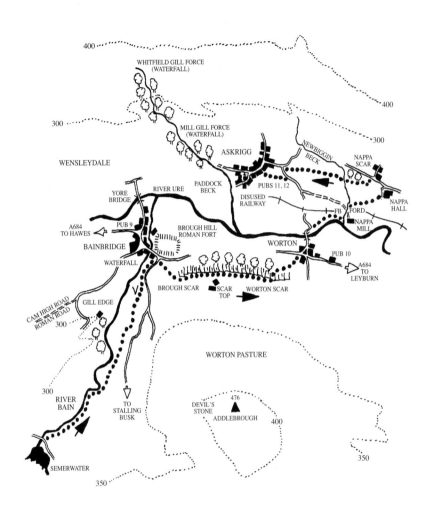

400

WHITFIELD GILL FORCE
(WATERFALL)

400

300

300

MILL GILL FORCE
(WATERFALL)

ASKRIGG

NEWBIGGIN BECK

NAPPA SCAR

WENSLEYDALE

PADDOCK BECK

PUBS 11, 12

YORE BRIDGE

RIVER URE

DISUSED RAILWAY

FB

FORD

NAPPA HALL

A684 TO HAWES

PUB 9

BROUGH HILL ROMAN FORT

NAPPA MILL

BAINBRIDGE

WORTON

PUB 10

WATERFALL

A684 TO LEYBURN

CAM HIGH ROAD
ROMAN ROAD

GILL EDGE

BROUGH SCAR

SCAR TOP

WORTON SCAR

300

WORTON PASTURE

300

RIVER BAIN

TO STALLING BUSK

DEVIL'S STONE

476

ADDLEBROUGH

400

350

SEMERWATER

350

MAP SIX

©Crown Copyright 2005. All rights reserved. Licence Number 100011978

CRAY is a tiny hamlet with a couple of old farmhouses, one or two cottages, some tumbledown barns and the White Lion Inn, Wharfedale's highest pub, which is situated alongside the road over to Bishopdale by way of the Kidstones Pass. This old drovers' inn dates back to the 17th Century and retains a great deal of character with flagstone floors and a large open fire dominating the bar. Centuries ago it would have been busy with travellers, drovers and packhorse men for the old packhorse route between Wensleydale and Wharfedale came this way before following what is now a footpath down alongside Cray Gill to cross the Wharfe over the bridge at Hubberholme. This old packhorse trail boasts a rare example of a medieval packhorse bridge across the side-stream of Crook Gill just to the south of Cray. This small bridge does not have any parapets thus allowing fully laden packhorses to cross it unhindered. Cray's main claim to fame are the spectacular series of waterfalls along Cray Gill, indeed the name of the hamlet dates back to the ancient tribes of pre-Roman Britain for Cray is a Celtic word that means 'fresh stream'. *"....Cray, its inn and single farmhouse perched solitary on the brink of a wooded, deep ravine. To sleep in this inn is to awake next morning to a sense of spacious ease. The air blows sweet from the massive bulk of Buckden Pike; and everywhere there is the roar and bubble of descending waters. Cray holds its own among all Wharfe's secluded corners, a hamlet instinct with peculiar charm. From the pasture lands above the inn, where grey, stone fences stride to the further skies, you look down-dale on Buckden."* (H. Sutcliffe 'The Striding Dales' 1929).

From Buckden a superb stony track, known as Buckden Rake, slants steeply up through Rakes Wood across the lower flanks of Buckden Pike then leads across the flat shelf of moorland above Cray before joining the track across Stake Moss towards Bainbridge in Wensleydale – this once formed part of the Roman road between the forts at Ilkley and Bainbridge. This walk is one of the most spectacular in all of England crossing wild moorland and desolate valleys that are the preserve of the walker. There is a particularly delightful spot to rest beside a small waterfall along Shaw Gate Gill – nothing but the sound of cascading water, bird song and bleating sheep with wonderful views across the remote valley of Cragdale.

"This green track is a walkers' way par excellence. The signpost says: 'Bainbridge'. Wisely, it omits the distance, for once you are on your way, you lose count of the miles; your measure is the succession of glorious panoramas which greet you, one after another, as you go with the wind across the wild uplands." (A. Wainwright 'A Pennine Journey - The Story of a Long Walk in 1938' 1986).

RAYDALE once formed part of the hunting forest of the Lords of Middleham Castle and means the 'valley of the roebuck'; indeed the name Stalling Busk can roughly be translated as the 'clearing in the forest for the stallions'. Raydale is a hidden side-valley, a tributary of Wensleydale. It is closed in by high fells including Yockenthwaite Moor (643 metres), Fleet Moss (596 metres) and Drumaldrace (614 metres), names that stir the imagination. These high fells often experiences sudden changes in weather; the first falls of snow in Wensleydale are often on Drumaldrace and Fleet Moss. Streams gather peaty waters from these moorland heights and tumble down through the wild valleys of Bardale, Raydale and Cragdale before converging on the flat, marshy pastures between Marsett and Stalling Busk, where Raydale opens out into a broad and beautiful valley. *"There is a crystallized beauty about this valley of Raydale, a perfection which is almost exotic."* (E. Pontefract & M. Hartley 'Wensleydale' 1936). Raydale was first settled by Scandinavian farmers over 1,000 years ago as the place-names testify – Marsett and Countersett are derived from the Old Norse word 'saetr' meaning 'summer pastures'.

STALLING BUSK, known locally as Busk, enjoys an elevated position at 1,100 feet above sea level (336m) and has good views across the dale; the locals say that Stalling Busk is on the money side of the dale whilst Marsett is on the sunny side. *"Frank Outhwaite told me 'They always used to say to the folk at Busk - you've to pay more to be on t'grandstand.' For two months of the year, the sun does not shine directly on Raydale House because 'it's that much under t'hill."* (W. R. Mitchell 'High Dale Country' 1991). The ruins of the old Parish Church of Stalling Bush stand in a beautiful location just above the still waters of Semerwater. This church was originally built in 1603 as a chapel of ease to serve the scattered communities of Raydale. It became a parish church in the 1860s and continued in use up until the early 20th Century when the new Church of St Matthew was built in the village in 1909. The old church then fell into disuse and became a ruin, although the churchyard is still used for burials; indeed, there are over 750 people buried in this churchyard. This ruinous building in such peaceful surroundings evokes a sense of eternal peace.

SEMERWATER has the distinction of being one of only three large natural sheets of water in Yorkshire, the others being Malham Tarn and Hornsea Mere. Its lovely setting even inspired Turner to paint it. Semerwater is not as grand as any of the Cumbrian lakes, but history and legend make it a fascinating place. *".... so I made a detour to see it....It is a flooded field."* **(A. Wainwright 1986).** Semerwater is a glacial lake, a remnant of the last Ice Age when a moraine of debris left by the retreating Wensleydale glacier held back melt waters. A river has now made a channel through this moraine to join Semerwater with the Ure; this is the River Bain, the shortest river in England. The lake is home to many different species of migratory birds and the surrounding marshland supports a great variety of rare plants, consequently the whole area has been designated as a Site of Special Scientific Interest. The Yorkshire Wildlife Trust manages 55 acres of this land as a nature reserve.

There are two legends associated with Semerwater. The first concerns the Carlow Stone, a large boulder of Shap granite brought down by the ice thousands of years ago that can be found on the shore of Semerwater. Geologically speaking, this boulder is a classic example of a glacial erratic; however, legend tells us that a giant was stood on top of Addlebrough and dropped the Carlow Stone as he hurled it at the Devil who was stood on Crag Hill across the valley. The Devil retaliated, however his stone fell short of the summit of Addlebrough; this stone is known as the Devil's Stone. An old local tradition is for couples to visit the stone soon after they have been engaged; touching the stone supposedly brings good fortune and many healthy children.

The second legend describes how once a large, prosperous and beautiful city stood where the lake is now. An angel, dressed as a poor

man, tried in vain to find a bed for the night. He eventually found a humble house on a hillside above the city in which a poor couple lived where he was fed and given a bed for the night. The next morning he thanked the couple and turned to the city in the distance and cried :-
'Semerwater rise, Semerwater sink,
And cover all save this li'le house
That gave me meat and drink.'

"Then the earth made a hissing noise, the stream grew into a large lake, and the city was no more. Yet unto this day the natives tell us that the roofs of the buried city are ofttimes seen deep down in the limpid waters." (**E. Bogg 'From Eden Vale to the Plains of York'**). There may be some truth in this because when the level of the lake was lowered in 1937 evidence of pile dwellings and Bronze and Iron Age artefacts were discovered.

BAINBRIDGE is a delightful village with a large green overlooked by a 15th Century inn. To complete the scene, there are a series of attractive waterfalls where the River Bain tumbles down limestone rock ledges, which can be viewed from the road bridge near to which are two old water-powered mills. *"We soon come to the broad and cheerful green, surrounded by a picturesque scattering of old but well preserved cottages; for Bainbridge has sufficient charms to make it a pleasant inland resort for holiday times that is quite ideal for those who are content to abandon the sea. The overflow from Semmerwater, which is called the Bain, fills the village with its music as it falls over ledges of rock in many cascades along one side of the green."* (**G. Home 'Yorkshire' 1908**). There is more to Bainbridge than meets the eye for its history stretches back almost two thousand years to the time of the Romans. In about AD80, legions of Roman soldiers pushed northwards from their military stronghold of Eboracum (York) to subdue the unruly native British Brigantes tribes. A network of roads and forts were built during this period under the supervision of Agricola, Rome's most successful governor in Britain. A fort, known as Virosidum, was built on Brough Hill which rises just to the east of Bainbridge. *"One of the loveliest views of the village is from Brough Hill...the site of the Roman fort. Looking east from the summit you see the grace of Wensleydale. It is* *worth while climbing it in the early morning after heavy rain for a sight of the flooded valley. It is a fine view-point, easily reached, which is probably why the Romans chose it."* (E. **Pontefract & M. Hartley 1936**). This fort housed up to 500 soldiers who kept a watchful eye on the local Brigantes for nearly 300 years, although it was attacked and rebuilt on several occasions. A number of Roman roads were built across the fells to this fort, including the impressive track of Cam High Road that once led across the hills to Ribchester, the course of which can still be seen cutting a straight line up across the flanks of Wether Fell. Our route from Buckden via Stake Moss follows the line of the Roman Road from Ilkley to Bainbridge. The wooded Brough Scar affords a bird's eye view of the classic 'playing card' shape of the Roman fort. *"Good was their choice, for with enemies on every side among the wild hills, it would be held impregnable, in spite of many desperate attempts made upon it, in fact, this district has been a stern battling-ground, and one can almost catch the sound of arms clashing and welling up from the aisles of old time."* (E. **Bogg 'Beautiful Wensleydale' 1925**).

In medieval times the large village green had an important purpose as a refuge for livestock as the village was then on the edge of the vast hunting Forest of Wensleydale that stretched from the River Bain to Mallerstang and was home to twelve foresters and their families. Wolves, wild boars and bears roamed the forest, while eagles soared above making it a dangerous place to be after dark, so much so that a law was passed which stated that a horn was to be blown every evening from the Feast of Holy Rood (September 27th) to Shrovetide to guide travellers to the safety of the village. This custom still remains today and the Bainbridge Forest Horn hangs in the passageway of the Rose & Crown. *"In the most savage recesses still lurked the bear, and the wild boar found a safe hiding place. At that period wolves were numerous, and woe to the benighted traveller if overtaken by a pack of those hungry animals. Herds of deer, and troops of half-wild hogs, and oxen inhabited the softer and more luxuriant glades by the river's brink...the forest horn is sounded, as a signal to the benighted travellers who may have lost their way amongst the mountains."* (E. **Bogg**). In 1663 villagers bought the manorial rights of Bainbridge from the City of London, this survives today in the form of the locally elected Lords Trustees of the Manor of Bainbridge whose main responsibility is the maintenance of the sprawling village green, complete with stocks. The 18th Century Yore Bridge that spans the River Ure was designed by the famous designer John Carr, who also designed Buxton's Crescent and Harewood House near Leeds, although his 'bread and butter' was bridges.

ADDLEBROUGH (480 metres) rises up to the south of Bainbridge, its distinctive profile and table-top summit instantly recognisable. Its flat summit plateau, characteristic of many hills in this part of the Yorkshire Dales, is due to the underlying Yoredale series of rocks. This rock strata consists of layers of limestone, grits and shales which are sandwiched together, each type of rock eroding at different rates resulting in the 'stepped' appearance of the valley sides as well as the many waterfalls and flat-topped hills. On its summit are traces of a prehistoric hill-fort and a large cairn beside which are two cup marked rocks, whilst on its southern flanks are the remains of a extensive Bronze Age settlement. This cairn is said to be the burial site of an ancient British chieftain called Authulf, who gave the hill its name – the word 'brough' indicates an ancient defensive site. The cup marked rocks are quite a rarity in the Yorkshire Dales. No one really knows the true meaning of these carvings; they could be fertility symbols, religious carvings or perhaps messages for other people as they are usually located on high ground, beside ancient trackways or important burial sites. It is thought that the Romans later used this defensive site as a lookout to help protect their fort on Brough Hill just to the east of Bainbridge far below in the valley.

WORTON, pronounced 'Werton', is a small hamlet situated along the main road through Wensleydale. A closer look will reveal some beautiful old houses including Worton Hall dated 1600 said to be the oldest house in Wensleydale. Worton's main claim to fame is the Bread Riot of 1757 when local people, annoyed at the high price of corn, attacked a delivery of corn that was destined for the more affluent gentlemen of the upper dale. The village pub, the Victoria Arms, is well worth the short diversion for this is one of the few remaining unspoilt pubs left in the Yorkshire Dales. This legendary pub has been run by Ralph and Pat Daykin since 1956. It is unique, a reminder of days gone by when country inns were a place where locals and travellers could relax in the comfort of the landlord's home. Income would often be supplemented by a smallholding; this pub is the last surviving example in the Yorkshire Dales of a farm-cum-pub.

NAPPA HALL was built circa 1450 by Thomas Metcalfe as a fortified house or 'pele tower' on 400 acres of land that had been given to his family by Sir Richard Scrope of Bolton Castle in the 15th Century for the bravery of James Metcalfe at the battle of Agincourt. Mary Queen of Scots reputedly stayed here for two nights whilst she was being held 'captive' at nearby Bolton Castle, and James the First also stayed here whilst on a hunting trip in nearby Raydale. *"A characteristic Wensleydale house is the fifteenth century Nappa Hall, overlooking the Ure near Askrigg, and characteristic of the district are its legends. Here Mary, Queen of Scots, spent two days on a visit to Sir Christopher Metcalfe, then head of the famous dale family to which Nappa belonged, and here her ghost is said to have been frequently seen – one of its appearances, in fact, was so real to a lady who was visiting the house at the time that she wrote a detailed account of the occurrence."* (**Fletcher 'Nooks & Corners of Yorkshire'**). The Metcalfes were a very important family in Wensleydale, holding important positions for generations, including High Sheriff of Yorkshire and Master Forester of the forests of Wensleydale; they even had their own chapel within Askrigg church. By the end of the 18th Century the Hall had fallen into disrepair and the power of the family had dwindled. After over 550 years of Metcalfe ownership, Nappa Hall was put up for sale in 2008, the first time in its history. In need of complete renovation, the hall is currently on English Heritage's 'Buildings at Risk' register. Thankfully, Nappa Hall has been bought by a someone who cares about its history and plans to renovate and live in it. The Metcalfe name has had a strong presence in Wensleydale since the 12th Century and continues to be a common surname today.

ASKRIGG is a fascinating place; to appreciate it fully you must spend time exploring. *"Askrigg seen from a distance is one of the pictures in Wensleydale which never lose their freshness....Seeing it in winter across the snow-covered valley, the walls of the houses show dark against the surrounding whiteness, like children in cosy caps, and only the cottage lights twinkling in the frosty air tell of its reality. From far and near there is an enchantment in the view, so that you enter Askrigg with anticipation. And you are not disappointed."* (**E. Pontefract & M. Hartley 1936**). 'Ascric', meaning 'ash ridge', was mentioned in the Doomsday book and grew as a trading centre on the edge of the old forest of Wensleydale as it lay just outside the forest boundaries and so was exempt from the strict Norman forest laws. Following the Norman Conquest, the Cistercian monks, under their charismatic leader Bernard of Clairvaux, came over from France and established small communities in wild and remote places where they could follow the strict rules of their Order – poverty, simplicity, spirituality and devotion to prayer. Within fifty years, they had established eight major abbeys throughout the North of England including Rievaulx, Fountains, Byland and Jervaulx. A monastery was built at Bowbridge, then known as Fors Abbey, just to the west of Askrigg as a daughter house of Byland Abbey, but the land was poor and the climate too harsh and so in 1156 they moved to the present site further down the valley along the banks of the River Ure where they established Jervaulx Abbey, which took its name from the Norman French word for valley 'vaulx' and 'Jer' from the old name for the River Ure 'Yore'. The present church, dedicated to St Oswald, dates from the mid 15th Century, although it stands on 13th Century foundations. This church was built to serve a growing settlement as well as several surrounding communities and is the largest church in Wensleydale. It retains many features including a fine 15th Century ceiling supported by huge beams as well as lead on its roof from local mines. During the medieval period, much of the surrounding land was owned by the monks of Jervaulx on which they grazed their vast flocks of sheep.

A market charter was granted in 1587, and the Lancaster to Richmond turnpike road came through Askrigg in 1751. However, by the mid 19th Century the market had lapsed and Hawes gradually began to take over as the 'capital' of the upper dale. Askrigg's heyday was in the 18th and early 19th Centuries when lead mining, textile production (Askrigg had three mills) and clock making was at its height. Clock making began in Askrigg in the early 17th Century, and lasted up until the last shop closed in 1936. Originally the clocks only had hour hands as the Dales people were not interested in minutes. The main street is lined with impressive Georgian and Victorian three-storey buildings, whilst by the church the street broadens into a small cobbled marketplace complete with a stepped market cross, all of which bears witness to its early growth as a prosperous market town rather than a rural village. Close to the market cross, with its bull-ring still set into the cobbles, stood Askrigg Old Hall. This Hall was built in 1678 and had a second floor wooden gallery which was used to watch the bull baiting below. Sadly this house, described as one of the treasures of Wensleydale, was destroyed by fire in 1935. *"....with it's many windows bearing an impress of some antiquated residence of bygone London".* **(E. Bogg).**

There are two spectacular waterfalls, Mill Gill Force and Whitfield Gill Force, a short distance from the centre of Askrigg, both of which are set in a steep-sided wooded ravine. These waterfalls are caused by the Yoredale Series of rocks, which are comprised of layers of sandstone, limestone, slates and mineral bearing rocks sandwiched together and therefore eroding at varying rates. *There is a beautiful walk from Askrigg to Mill Gill Force. The distance is scarcely more than half a mile across sloping pastures and through the curious stiles that appear in the stone walls. So dense is the growth of trees in the little ravine that one hears the sound of the waters close at hand without seeing anything but the profusion of foliage overhanging and growing among the rocks. After climbing down among the moist ferns and moss-grown stones, the gushing cascades appear suddenly set in a frame of such lavish beauty that they hold a high place among their rivals in the dale."* **(G. Home 1908).** To reach the falls follow the lane past St Oswald's Church, *"....a ramble among the tombs will afford epitaphs of an eccentric character. One, for example, to the memory of Myles Alderson, who died in 1746, states that he was 'an honest attorney'."* **(W. Andrews 'Picturesque Yorkshire').** Askrigg has the distinction of being the first village in Yorkshire and one of the first in England to be lit by electricity; power was generated by a turbine attached to one of the mill wheels, *"-Ye Gods ! - by the Lightning's applied force - Electricity".* **(E. Bogg 1925).** In the 1970s and 80s Askrigg was used as the setting for the TV series 'All Creatures Great and Small' with the Kings Arms doubling as the 'Drovers' whilst the grand three-storey house near the Market Cross was used as 'Skeldale House'. All of this combines together to make Askrigg the finest village in the Yorkshire Dales.

ASKRIGG
to
REETH

✦

*"Every person has a favourite place where they linger; this may be a
deserted beach, a mountain peak or the centre of a bustling city. For me
this place is Swaledale. No where in the world can rival its rugged
beauty. Majestic fells sweep down to meet the bubbling, cascading river,
hidden gills beckon you to explore their secrets and time mellowed stone
villages complement the scenery to perfection. To stand on the flanks of
Kisdon Hill and look out across the rooftops of Muker towards Gunnerside
fills you with a sense of well being and fulfilment which is beyond words
– you have to experience it. And once you have you will be totally
captivated by the overwhelming splendour of Swaledale."*

Mark Reid 1995

WALK INFORMATION

Points of interest:	Wild Oxnop Ghyll, a haunted bridge, the Corpse Way, traditional hay meadows, Viking settlements, the legacy of the lead mining industry, hidden treasure and probably the most beautiful valley in the world.

Distance:

Askrigg to Gunnerside	6 miles
Gunnerside to Reeth	7 miles
Total	13 miles

Time: Allow 7 hours

Terrain: The section from Askrigg to Ivelet Bridge follows exposed moorland roads and tracks over Askrigg Common and Satron Moor and then down through Oxnop Ghyll; much of this follows unenclosed moorland roads. The initial climb out of Askrigg is long and quite steep in places. From Ivelet Bridge, clear paths lead across meadowland and along the banks of the River Swale to Gunnerside (firm ground). The section from Gunnerside to Reeth crosses meadowland, rough pastures and heather moorland, with a steady climb up across rough fields (boggy in places) from Haverdale Beck to Birks End Farm. The path is not clearly defined in places and can be exposed to the elements, especially on Harkerside Moor (long grass or heather, sometimes boggy). The final approach to Reeth crosses the River Swale by way of the Swing Bridge (footbridge).

Take care walking along the moorland road between Askrigg and Oxnop Ghyll. Please walk in single file across meadowland. There is a shallow ford across Haverdale Beck, which may be difficult after heavy rain.

Ascents:	Askrigg Common:	500 metres
	Harkerside Moor:	370 metres

Viewpoints:	The climb out of Askrigg affords good views over Askrigg and Wensleydale.
	Descent through Oxnop Ghyll looking across Swaledale.
	View from the road near to Bank Heads Farm and also Birks End Farm.
	Descent from Harkerside Moor towards Reeth.

FACILITIES

Askrigg	Inn / B&B / Shop / Café / Bus / Phone / Toilets
Ivelet	Phone
Gunnerside	Inn / B&B / Café / Bus / Phone / Toilets
Reeth	Inn / B&B / Shop / P.O. / Café / Bus / Phone / Toilets / Info. / Camp

ROUTE DESCRIPTION

(Map Seven)

From the centre of Askrigg, head up along the main street then take the turning to the left towards 'Muker' just after the Crown Inn. Follow this road up out of the village and follow it climbing steeply up (ignore the turning to the right by the two stone barns) onto Askrigg Common to reach a cattle grid across the road after just over a mile (at the end of the walled road - open moorland ahead). After the cattle grid, follow the unfenced moorland road straight on gently rising up across Askrigg Common - the road soon levels out and continues on meandering across the moor to reach another cattle grid after 0.75 miles. Carry straight on along the road for a further 0.25 miles then, where the road forks ('chevron' road sign) follow the right-hand narrow lane straight on, with Oxnop Ghyll falling away to your left (SD 939 944). Follow this rough, unenclosed lane straight on for approx. 0.5 miles to reach a gate in a wall across the lane, with the impressive crags of Oxnop Scar just to your left *(caution – sheer drops)*. Head through the gate and continue along this quiet unenclosed lane for a further 1.5 miles passing through four more gates skirting across the eastern flanks of Oxnop Ghyll gradually winding down towards Swaledale to reach a fifth gate across the road *(NB gate missing)* just after Gill Head Farm (stone farmhouse just down to your left). After this fifth gate (gate missing) continue along the road for approx. 50 yards then take the footpath to the left through a small wall-gate (SP) - SD 934 971. Walk straight on down across the field bearing slightly to the right (head towards the telegraph pole in the centre of the field) to reach a small wall-gate, then straight on down across the field to join the road through another small wall-gate. Turn left along the road then almost immediately right down alongside Oxnop Beck to reach Ivelet Bridge across the River Swale.

(Map Eight)

Cross Ivelet Bridge and follow the road to the right alongside the river at first then rising up into the hamlet of Ivelet. Turn right at the telephone box (SP 'Gunnerside') along a lane passing in front of some stone houses on your left then, at the end of the houses, drop down over a FB across Shore Gill and up to a wall-gate. After this wall-gate follow the clear path ahead across several fields through a series of narrow wall-gaps. After approx. 0.5 miles the path runs along the top of a steep bank above the River Swale then gently drops down alongside a fence on your right to reach a stile over a fence at the bottom of the hill. Turn left here (away from the river) across more fields through wall-gaps to reach Gunnerside. Follow the lane straight on between the houses to reach the main road in the centre of the village opposite the bridge across Gunnerside Beck (SD 951 982).

Turn right along this main road (road sign 'Muker, Kirkby Stephen') and follow this down to reach Gunnerside New Bridge across the River Swale. Cross the bridge then follow the road bending up to the right and round to the left then, where the road bends right again, turn left along the road (road sign 'Crackpot') over a cattle grid beside a metal gate, after which the road divides – take the left-hand track down through a gate (SP 'Grinton'). Follow the track down passing some green caravans (screened behind trees) just after which head through a double metal gate in fence on your right (SP 'Bank Heads'). After the gate, head left across the middle of the field and through a gap in the wall then follow the well-marked path straight ahead through more wall-gaps and over stiles for approx. 0.75 miles until Bank Heads Farm appears up to your right. Head to the right across the field (heading towards the farm) and through a gate in the field corner (SP), after which follow the grassy track up towards the farm then through a wall-gap to the right of the farm than leads onto the road (SD 962 973). Turn left along the road for 0.75 miles passing a handful of cottages/farms (ignore the first FP to the left after about 0.5 miles) then passing the entrance to Mudd House (with its cattle grid) and continue along the road for a short distance then take the FP to the left through a small wall-gate (SP) just above Mudd House. After the wall-gate, head to the right across fields through a series of small wall-gates then, as you cross the last undulating field, head straight on (ignore the wall-gate towards the bottom left corner of this field) to join the road (SD 976 969).

Turn left along the road then almost immediately right (back on yourself) through a gate (SP 'Footpath only, No vehicles') down along a clear track that leads through woodland to reach a shallow ford and a FB across Haverdale Beck above some impressive waterfalls. After the FB, turn left across the field to quickly reach a wall-gate then head straight on across the next field (ignore wall gate to the left) to reach another wall-gate. After this wall-gate, continue straight on across the hillside over a stile (and wall-gap immediately beyond it) then bear right up the rough hillside to reach a small wall-gate set in a 'dog leg' in the wall at the top of the field, after which continue on bearing slightly to the right up across the middle of the field and through another wall-gate to the right of a stone barn. After this wall-gate, head straight on bearing very slightly to the left across the field (heading towards Hops House ahead), through a small wall-gate (10 yards to the left of the shallow drainage ditch in the middle of the field) then up to reach Hops House Farm. Head through the gate immediately to the right of the farmhouse and then walk through the farmyard (passing in front of the house) then, at the end of the yard, cross the stone FB beside the ford immediately after which head through the wall-gap directly ahead (do not continue along the track). After the wall-gap, bear to the right up across the field to reach the ruins of Birks End then, as you reach the ruins, pass to the left behind the old barns and over a stony ford across Birks Gill to join a walled grassy/stony track. Turn right up along this track, through a bridlegate then up alongside the boulder-strewn stream (Birks Gill) to reach the road beside a bridge (SD 987 967).

(Map Nine)

Turn left along the road and follow this on for just over 0.25 miles then, where the road bends round to the left, head through the gate to the right (BW). Follow the grassy track straight on through a further 8 gates heading across the flat 'shelf' of land on the lower flanks of High Carl. Keep heading straight on across the rough grassy hillside then, after the 9th gate since the road (wooden bridlegate in a wall), the terrain changes to rough heather/bilberry moorland − carry straight on along a narrow meandering path bearing very slightly to the right across the moorland (Harkerside Moor) to reach a gate in a wall towards the top of the field (marked by a solitary tree). After the gate, continue straight on across Browna Gill (small stream) along a rough grassy track over heather moorland for 0.25 miles to join a very clear gravel shooters' track coming down the hillside (SE 012 976). Turn left along this track and follow it all the way down to reach the road. Turn right along the road for 0.5 miles to reach the entrance to Harkerside Place Farm (SP 'Reeth via Swing Bridge'). Turn left down along the stony track towards the farm, over a cattle grid and into the farmyard − as you enter the farmyard take the first turning to the right along a clear farm track (SP). Follow this track on then, where the track forks after about 200 yards, head to the left through a gate in the wall just before another stone farmhouse (SP 'Grinton Swing

Bridge'). Bear to the right down across the field (do not head along the stony track) through a small wall-gate, after which head diagonally down across the field through another wall-gate then down to reach the large Swing Bridge over the River Swale (SE 032 989). Cross the bridge, turn right and follow the clear path across fields then, as you reach a large meander in the river, head over a small FB across boggy ground then follow the clear enclosed path up to the left to join the end of a lane which you follow to the right into Reeth.

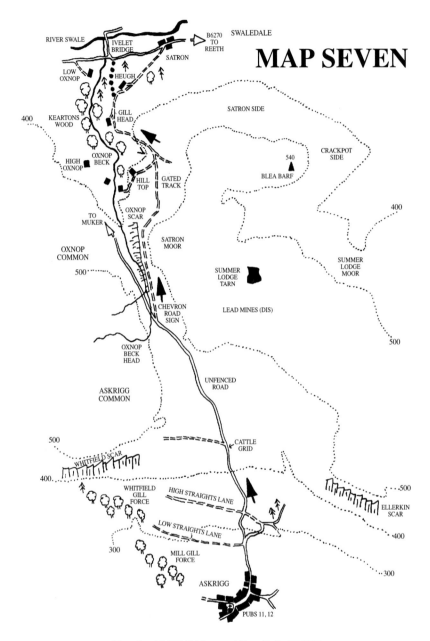

MAP SEVEN

©Crown Copyright 2005. All rights reserved. Licence Number 100011978

MAP EIGHT

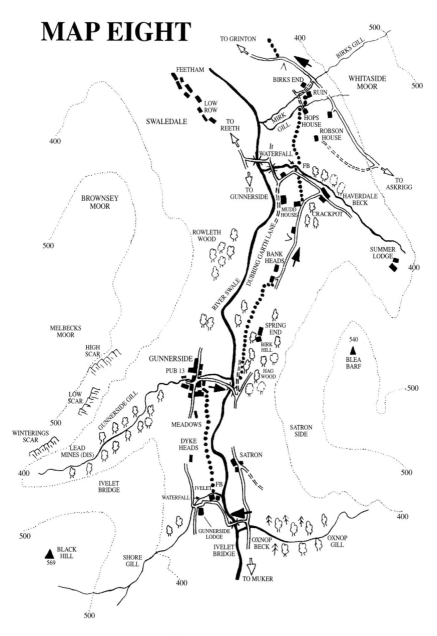

TO GRINTON

400

500

BIRKS GILL

FEETHAM

BIRKS END

WHITASIDE MOOR

500

RUIN

LOW ROW

MIRK GILL

HOPS HOUSE

SWALEDALE

TO REETH

ROBSON HOUSE

400

WATERFALL

FB

TO ASKRIGG

TO GUNNERSIDE

HAVERDALE BECK

BROWNSEY MOOR

MUDD HOUSE

CRACKPOT

ROWLETH WOOD

DUBBING GARTH LANE

BANK HEADS

SUMMER LODGE

500

400

RIVER SWALE

MELBECKS MOOR

SPRING END

540

HIGH SCAR

BIRK HILL

BLEA BARF

GUNNERSIDE

HAG WOOD

PUB 13

LOW SCAR

GUNNERSIDE GILL

500

500

MEADOWS

SATRON SIDE

WINTERINGS SCAR

DYKE HEADS

LEAD MINES (DIS)

SATRON

400

500

IVELET BRIDGE

IVELET

FB

WATERFALL

500

BLACK HILL

569

SHORE GILL

GUNNERSIDE LODGE

IVELET BRIDGE

OXNOP BECK

OXNOP GILL

400

400

TO MUKER

500

©Crown Copyright 2005. All rights reserved. Licence Number 100011978

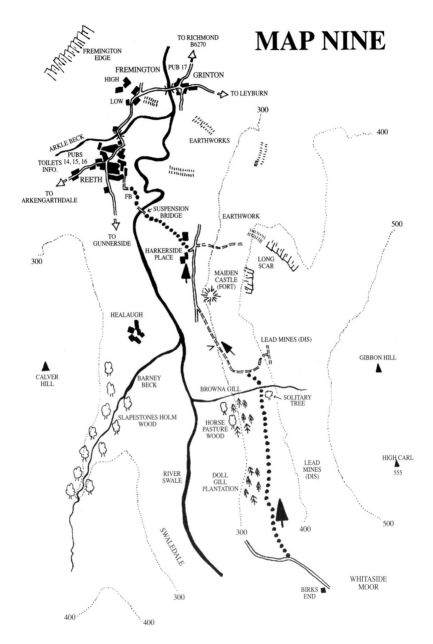

MAP NINE

TO RICHMOND
B6270

FREMINGTON
EDGE

FREMINGTON   PUB 17

HIGH   GRINTON

LOW   TO LEYBURN

300

400

ARKLE BECK

PUBS
TOILETS 14, 15, 16
INFO.

REETH

TO
ARKENGARTHDALE

FB

EARTHWORKS

300

SUSPENSION
BRIDGE

TO
GUNNERSIDE

HARKERSIDE
PLACE

EARTHWORK

500

LONG
SCAR

MAIDEN
CASTLE
(FORT)

HEALAUGH

LEAD MINES (DIS)

GIBBON HILL

CALVER
HILL

BARNEY
BECK

BROWNA GILL

SOLITARY
TREE

SLAPESTONES HOLM
WOOD

HORSE
PASTURE
WOOD

HIGH CARL

555

RIVER
SWALE

DOLL
GILL
PLANTATION

LEAD
MINES
(DIS)

300

400

500

SWALEDALE

WHITASIDE
MOOR

BIRKS
END

300

400   400

©Crown Copyright 2005. All rights reserved. Licence Number 100011978

OXNOP GILL is a little known tributary of Swaledale (pronounced 'Swardill' locally) that cuts a deep cleft into Satron Moor between the high fells of Lovely Seat and Blea Barf. This ravine boasts magnificent limestone scenery, including the impressive sheer crags of Oxnop Scar at the head of the valley *"....my own road was taking me rapidly down into the valley, through a rocky boulder-strewn gorge with a most impressive wall of crags above on the right."* **(A. Wainwright 'A Pennine Journey - The Story of a Long Walk in 1938' 1986).** This road was once a busy route between the two dales; indeed, a popular wayside inn known as 'Jenkin Gate' once stood near to the cattle grid on the moorland road which was popular with the local mining community and passing travellers. The whole walk from Askrigg to Ivelet is an absolute delight with far-reaching views across Wensleydale from Askrigg Common that takes in, on a clear day, Great Whernside, Buckden Pike, Addlebrough, Raydale, Semerwater and much of Wensleydale – breathe in deeply and capture this swathe of England in your mind's eye forever. Expansive moorland soon gives way to the rich greens of Swaledale, with views of this wonderful valley opening up with every step. *"Swaledale was in front now, unfolding a little more of its beauty with every step I took......I could see copse and woodland, rich meadow and pleasant pasture wonderfully blended in the shades of soaring hill and ragged peak, and my heart warmed at the sight."* **(A. Wainwright 1986).** There are some good examples of long-house farms in Oxnop, which were designed so that house and barn are all under the same roof. This building style dates back to the Vikings; many Norse traditions, place names and farming techniques survive in one form or another in the upper reaches of the dales, *"It is said that up until the sixteenth century a Norse speech lingered in the remoter corners of Upper Swaledale and Wensleydale, strongly enough for a dalesman to have made himself understood to a Norwegian."* **(E. Pontefract & M. Hartley 'Yorkshire Tour' 1939).** The dialect in the area today is still strong and contains many words associated with Old Norse.

SWALEDALE is perhaps the most beautiful of all of Yorkshire's dales, where you will find Nature at its best. There are high mountains at the head of the valley whose evocative names such as Great Shunner Fell and Rogan's Seat echo the voices of the Vikings who settled there over 1,000 years ago. From its source high on the fells of High Seat, sparkling moorland streams cascade down through small ravines to swell the waters of Birkdale Beck, which soon meet the waters of Great Sleddale Beck that rises on the flanks of Great Shunner Fell. This confluence of becks creates one of Yorkshire's great rivers – the Swale. The river now rushes towards Keld where it tumbles over a series of spectacular waterfalls before sweeping round the 'island' hill of Kisdon, hemmed in by towering slopes and limestone crags. At Muker, the valley broadens slightly with flat riverside pastures criss-crossed by an intricate web of drystone walls and dotted with stoutly-built barns; this is the classic Yorkshire Dales landscape. On either side, the steep slopes sweep up to the moorland heights that are touched by wild sternness, the preserve of hardy Swaledale sheep and red grouse. Over generations, dales folk have shaped and modified this landscape and left a legacy of history, folklore and legend. The hills tell a tale of a lead mining industry that began with the Romans. There are ruined monastic buildings, ancient churches, packhorse bridges, attractive villages and old-fashioned country pubs, not to mention the Old Norse place-names and Swaledale dialect. *"Neither Arkengarthdale nor Swaledale have yet been fully discovered by tourists. That is their loss, for Swaledale is one of the proudest possessions of the county. The good road that winds the length of the dale, now climbing, now dropping, ever crossing and recrossing the turbulent Swale, provides country that is a veritable feast for the eye."* (J. &.R Fairfax-Blakeborough 'The Spirit of Yorkshire' 1954.)

IVELET BRIDGE spans the River Swale, the fastest flowing river in England. This is one of the best examples of a packhorse bridge in the Yorkshire Dales with a single, graceful high arch, *"...like a rainbow set in stone."* (W. Mitchell 'High Dale Country' 1991). The bridge, which was probably built in the 16th Century, is also steeped in history and legend. The 'Corpse Way' passes the bridge en route from Keld to Grinton. Before a church was built at Muker in 1580 the people of the upper dale had to carry their dead to the burial ground at Grinton, a 12 mile journey that took two days to complete. This journey originally stemmed from Norse mythology in which the 'corpse way' mirrored the last journey of the soul from earth to the next life. The dead were carried in wicker baskets and wrapped in a shroud, stone slabs were placed along the route on which the coffin could be rested, an example of which survives today at the north end of Ivelet Bridge. *"At Riddings Farm, near Feetham, a barn still known as Dead House is pointed out as the place where mourners would often leave their burden overnight; this gave them a chance to spend a convivial evening at the neighbouring Punch Bowl Inn."* (**G. B. Wood 'Yorkshire Tribute' 1950**) - well, why not? The bridge is reputedly haunted by a headless black dog, which will bring misfortune if you see it. *"The dog was always seen gliding on to the bridge, where it would disappear over the edge."* (**E. Pontefract & M. Hartley 'Swaledale' 1934**). The tiny hamlet of Ivelet is dominated by the imposing Gunnerside Lodge, a shooting lodge once owned by Lord Peel.

The finest hay-meadows in the Yorkshire Dales, arguably in England, can be found in Upper Swaledale, in particular around Keld, Muker, Ivelet and Gunnerside. In spring and early summer the small fields along the flat valley floor are not the ubiquitous dark green of 'improved' fields but a mass of bright yellows, blues, reds and whites gently swaying in the breeze with over twenty different species of wild flowers and grasses such as buttercup, forget-me-not, cow parsley, clover, common bird's-foot trefoil and meadow cranesbill. These meadows are cut later than normal to allow the wild flowers and grasses time to seed. To walk through these in mid June is an experience not to be missed. *"It makes an unforgettable Alpine-like picture, and once you have seen it no amount of grey weather can efface it from your mind."* (**E. Pontefract & M. Hartley 1939**).

GUNNERSIDE originated as a small Norse farming settlement as the steep fells and narrow valley floor would have reminded those early settlers of home. It was a Viking chieftain called Gunnar who first settled here in around the 10th Century and gave his name to his upland summer pastures, which the Vikings called 'saetrs'. Over the centuries, this name has evolved and is used as a suffix in many place-names throughout the Yorkshire Dales such as Lovely Seat, Marsett and Gunnerside. The Vikings brought with them a system of farming that is still essentially in use today. They grazed their livestock in the sheltered valleys during spring and autumn, and then moved them to higher pastures (the 'saetrs') during the summer months, leaving the grass to grow in the valley for use as winter fodder. Over time, these valley pastures became enclosed by stone walls, with a barn for each field where hay could be stored and cows housed during winter, whilst the high fells remained unenclosed common land. The fields to the east of Gunnerside stand as some of the best examples of this type of farming in the Yorkshire Dales with a jumble of small fields, each with its own stone barn.

Gunnerside remained virtually unchanged until the development of the lead mining industry on the moors and in the side-valleys behind the village in the 18th Century. Lead mining in the Dales can be traced back to Roman times and continued through the centuries, albeit on a small-scale, particularly by the monks of medieval England. After the Dissolution of the Monasteries new wealthy landowners developed the mines on a larger scale aided by advancements in technology, which resulted in the heyday of lead mining in the Yorkshire Dales between 1790 and 1860 when levels were driven deep into the hillsides, large smelting mills were built in the many side-valleys and miners' cottages swamped former farming villages. During this period around 6,000 tons of lead was produced annually in Swaledale. Lead from these Swaledale mines was used as early as the 12th Century to roof French abbeys and the King's Castle at Windsor; many cathedrals in Rome and castles in Germany have Swaledale lead on their roofs. Much of this mining activity took place in Gunnerside Gill, a steep-sided valley that cuts deeply into Melbecks Moor and Gunnerside Moor to the north of the village. A walk up through this ravine reveals a vast open-air museum to this once-flourishing but now forgotten industry. Ruinous crushing mills and old buildings litter the landscape whilst the hillsides are scarred with spoil heaps, flooded levels and hushes. Hushes are deep gashes in the hillside created by lead miners in search of a vein. They would build a small dam and flood the upper reaches of the ravine and then breach the dam sending a torrent of water down the hillside stripping away the vegetation thus, hopefully, revealing a rich vein of ore-bearing rock. These industrial scars add texture and history to the landscape and are now an integral part of the Yorkshire Dales. *"The men worked under conditions which would not be allowed to-day. They descended the shafts in complete darkness by ladders on either side, the last man pulling the door to after him....One man was not careful to knock all the snow from his clogs, and as he shut the door behind him he slipped and hurtled to the bottom."* **(E. Pontefract & M. Hartley 1934).** By the end of the 19th Century competition from abroad and dwindling reserves caused the demise of this industry and the miners cottages fell into disrepair; however the increasing popularity of Swaledale as a tourist centre has given a new lease of life to them as holiday homes. There is, however, one unique reminder of this almost forgotten industry. Calvert's Blacksmith's Shop is still in business, as it has been since the early 19th Century when it supplied the mines with tools and equipment. It is a rare survivor and remains completely unaltered with old lead mining implements hanging around the furnace and even a casting mould for the pigs of lead still with its inscription of 'Old Gang'.

I recommend that you take time to explore the village as there is more to Gunnerside than meets the eye. It lies astride the tumbling waters of Gunnerside Beck, a cluster of old miners' cottages and workshops that seem to have changed little since the days of the lead mines, huddled together around small 'greens' as if for protection against the elements and the harsh surroundings. The houses are functional rather than pretty, and there is a melancholy feeling about the place, a slight sense of sadness that is often found in villages once busy with industrial activity. Look into the heart of the village and you will see an active community with school, chapel, pub and cafe. *"But all beyond Reeth is a wilderness of hill, moor, torrent, crag, and heather-clad expanse. In summer the becks and waterfalls, each with its setting of grey rock and green fern, are haunts of beauty and of music; in winter, when the waters come pouring down from the hills in mighty torrents they are apt to strike awe into the hearts of folk who have never seen anything but a placid river."* (Fletcher 'Nooks & Corners of Yorkshire').

CRACKPOT is a small farming hamlet whose curious name comes from the Old Norse words meaning 'ravine where crows abound'. Swaledale is famous for its waterfalls, *"In Swaledale it is always the sound of falling water which call back one's wandering thoughts. I have paused to rest beside a little stream of wondrous beauty. Across the field, where two or three ashes grew together in a clump, I first saw it gleaming silver in the shadow; and a little lower down it ran beneath a bridge in the prettiest cascade imaginable. The fall was of trifling height, no more than three or four feet; but the water shot over it in a curve so full and copious and fell into so brown a pool below, beneath banks so cool and mossy, that there was more delight in watching it than one finds in many a stream of far greater volume."* (**A. Norway** 'Highways and Byways in Yorkshire' 1899). There is an impressive waterfall set in a wooded ravine along Haverdale Beck near to Crackpot. The name 'haverdale' means the 'valley where oats are grown' in Old Norse. Indeed, a havercake is an oatmeal bread cake that was once a Yorkshire staple, and is still enjoyed by many people throughout the county.

MAIDEN CASTLE lies hidden away on heather-clad Harkerside Moor, one of the most enigmatic prehistoric sites in Yorkshire. Built during the Iron Age over 2,000 years ago by the Brigantes tribes, this defensive site features an impressively deep earthwork rampart with an eastern entrance protected by parallel stone walls that extend for some 100 yards, giving it an unusual banjo shape. No one is sure why it was built and what purpose it served for it is unlikely to have been a defensive hill-fort for there is higher ground just to the south of the site that would have exposed it to attack. More probably, it was used as a ceremonial or religious site, which may explain the strange parallel stone walls. Some historians believe that the site was later used by the Romans as a look-out post and halting place as the Roman road between their forts at Bainbridge and Greta Bridge crossed the Swale near to Isles Bridge There are many more Iron Age defensive ditches and earthworks around Grinton and across Harkerside Moor, which are contemporary to Maiden Castle and may have been part of an extensive defensive system to protect the local lead mines from the advancing Roman legions. There are also two tumulus (prehistoric burial mounds) close to Maiden Castle, under one of which is reputedly buried a fortune in gold. *"Tradition has it that a chest of gold lies buried under the first mound, and many have searched for it. We found an old spade on one side with its edges curled over, which might have been left by some disconsolate digger."* (**E. Pontefract & M. Hartley 1934**). Maiden Castle can be found about 200 yards up to the right on the heather moorland where the gravel track and the road meet after the descent from Harkerside Moor. It is worth the detour for the earthworks are impressive and the views extensive, a thought-provoking place indeed.

The walk from Maiden Castle to Reeth is a delight, with an exciting crossing of the River Swale by way of the Swing Bridge. This bridge was re-built in 2002 after it had been washed away in floods two years earlier. The Swale is the fastest flowing river in England and can rise an amazing 10-feet in 20 minutes; indeed, the name Swale means 'rushing river' in Old English

REETH occupies a commanding position on the flanks of Calver Hill at the point where Arkengarthdale and Swaledale meet, indeed its name is derived from the Old English word for 'place at the stream'. Evidence of prehistoric occupation abounds in this area, particularly around nearby Fremington and Grinton with its ancient earthworks and defensive sites. Reeth's slightly elevated position would have proved more favourable for settlement, so that by the time of the Norman Conquest there was most probably a small village here, although the focal point for worship, originally pagan and then Christian, remained at Grinton. *"...Reeth, a small and picturesque town lying at the foot of Calver Hill and surrounded on all sides by wild and wide-spreading moors, claims to be the capital of Swaledale.....It is at this point that Swaledale becomes as savage in its scenery as the most desolate of Highland glens. Standing on Calver Hill one may look across a truly* *impressive stretch of dale and moor. The valley of the Swale lies in front..."* **(Fletcher).** Following the Norman Conquest, much of Upper Swaledale as well as Arkengarthdale was used by the lords of Richmond Castle as a hunting forest, with a hunting lodge built at Healaugh just to the west of Reeth. A number of cattle farms, known as 'vaccaries' were established within this forest, often on the site of existing Saxon or Norse farmsteads. These vaccaries were owned either by the lord of the manor or another large landowner, although some were gifted to monasteries and so became granges; a number of these vaccaries later grew into hamlets or villages. Small-scale lead mining in Swaledale can be traced back to Roman times, and this continued throughout the medieval period under the control of monastic houses who owned tracts of land throughout Swaledale. Bridlington Priory held lands around Grinton, Rievaulx Abbey owned lands around Muker whilst the smaller nunneries at Marrick and Ellerton also held land. Throughout this medieval period Reeth remained a small farming settlement.

Following the Dissolution of the Monasteries in the early 16th Century, these monastic lands were taken by the Crown and subsequently sold to wealthy landowners as small manors. In the mid 16th Century, Lord Wharton became lord of the manors of Muker and Healaugh, which included Reeth. It was Phillip Lord Wharton, the fourth Lord Wharton, who changed the lives of the people of Swaledale and the face of the landscape in the late 17th Century when he developed coal and lead mining on his vast estates throughout Swaledale. Lord Wharton was a friend of Cromwell as well as a leading politician and Protestant dissenter who championed Nonconformist worship, the legacy of which continues to this day throughout Swaledale. He was also instrumental in gaining a market charter for Reeth in 1695. The village prospered during the 18th and 19th Centuries as a centre for lead mining and hand-knitting, which thrived in the dale during this period. The large square 'green' was probably laid out at this time to facilitate the new weekly market, new businesses and growing population. The many fine Georgian buildings which line the spacious green testify to this growth, in particular High Row with its three-storey buildings which give this corner of Reeth an urban feel reminiscent of an old North Riding market town. Here you will find the Kings Arms, a wonderfully proportioned inn that was built in 1734 and boasts a superb inglenook fireplace in the bar. A few doors away is the Black Bull Hotel which dominates High Row, a rambling old building that has expanded over the years to incorporate a former draper's shop, whose beautiful Georgian shopfront can still be seen – note the unusual pub sign, the result of an old planning dispute with the National Park. The Half Moon juts out from High Row, another old pub that called last orders in 1911 and now used as holiday cottages. During the lead mining boom years, Reeth supported many more inns than it does today and was, by all accounts, like the Wild West on a Saturday night when the miners were in town! In its heyday Reeth supported seven fairs, a weekly market and a population three times greater than that of today; there were even plans to extend the branch line from Richmond to bring the railway to Reeth. However, by the end of the 19th Century the mines had closed and many people left for work in the cotton mills of Lancashire or the coal pits of Newcastle. The old cobbled market place between High Row and the large sloping green has recently been restored and the weekly Friday market revived, whilst the September Reeth Show still flourishes. *"It must have thrived with the lead-mines in Arkengarthdale and along the Swale, for it has gone back since the period of its former prosperity, and is glad of the fact that its situation, and the cheerful green which the houses look upon, have made it something of a holiday resort."* (**G. Home 'Yorkshire' 1908**).

Reeth has matured and mellowed over the years into what could be described as the perfect English country village; a large sloping village green surrounded by ancient inns, greystone houses and shops with enticing alleys leading off the green beckoning you to explore, all in a wonderful setting of river and moorland with the dramatic scars of Fremington Edge above Arkengarthdale dominating the scene and Calver Hill rising up behind the village; Reeth is the jewel in the crown of Swaledale. *"Clustering round the spacious green on a sunny slope are the grey old houses and inns of this little Swaledale town,... From the peace memorial on the green we see all the grandeur of its setting, with woooded hills and bare moorland heights on every hand, their heads often lost in clouds."* **(A. Mee 'Yorkshire North Riding' 1941).** The Swaledale Folk Museum, which is housed in the old Methodist Sunday School, is well worth a visit to see the many lead mining and farming implements of by-gone days and to gain an insight into local history. Reeth was James Herriot's 'Darrowby' in the film version of 'It Shouldn't Happen to a Vet'; the imposing house in the north-west corner of the green was 'Skeldale House' and the Black Bull doubled as the 'Drover's Arms'.

ARKENGARTHDALE is Yorkshire's most northerly dale, a landscape of stark beauty with wild moors, deep ravines, tumbling streams, crumbling lead mines, scattered farms and small villages clustered together for protection against the elements. Its unusual name originates from 'Arkil's garth'; 'Arkil' being the Norse chieftain in the area and 'garth' being his clearing. The road, which winds up the dale, passes many small hamlets with weird and wonderful names most of which are derived from Old Norse including Langthwaite, Eskeleth, Whaw, Faggergill and Punchard. The narrow road eventually reaches the lonely Tan Hill Inn, Britain's highest Inn at 1,732 feet above sea level, set amidst a vast landscape of wild moorland. The fells are scarred with more remains of the lead mining industry than any other dale as Arkengarthdale was once one of the most important and productive areas in Britain for lead mining, especially during the 18th and 19th Centuries. The numerous old spoil heaps, mine shafts, cottages and moorland tracks are reminders of this early contribution to the Industrial Revolution; these remains add to the sombre beauty of the area. *"The high road running through the dale by way of William Gill and Polly Moss leads to as lonely and desolate a tract of country as any one fond of solitude could desire - as lonely as (if not lonelier than) the moors of Bowes and Stainmore, to which it leads."* **(Fletcher).**

STAGE FOUR

REETH
to
WEST BURTON

✦

"I think the exact moment when it dawned on me that Yorkshire was a magical place was when I pulled my car off the unfenced road which leads from Leyburn over Bellerby Moor to Grinton. It was around the highest point, by a little stream, and I looked back over the swelling moorland to the great wooded valley of the Swale where it curves on its approach to Richmond. I gazed at the scene in disbelief. There was everything here; wildness and solitude breathing from the bare fells, yet a hint of softness where the river wound along the valley floor. And in all the green miles around me there was not another human being to be seen. I got out of my car and sat on the springy grass as I have done on countless occasions since then. I was captivated, completely spellbound and I still am to this day."

J. Herriot
'My Yorkshire' 1979.

WALK INFORMATION

. . . .

Points of interest: The 'Cathedral of the Dales', Apedale and Gibbon Hill, the castle where Mary Queen of Scots was held prisoner, Herriot's honeymoon hotel, Garibaldi's red shirts, spectacular waterfalls and the prettiest village in the Yorkshire Dales.

Distance:

Reeth to Carperby	8 miles
Carperby to West Burton	3 miles
Total	11 miles

Time: Allow 5 hours
(excluding stops at Bolton Castle and Aysgarth)

Terrain: Between Reeth and Castle Bolton the route predominantly follows clear gravel/turf tracks, with some sections along an unfenced moorland road – the climb up from Grinton to the top of Greets Hill is long and steady, whilst the climb out of Apedale over to Castle Bolton follows a superb grassy track with wonderful views. The section from Castle Bolton to Carperby follows field paths and heads through two farmyards, with some muddy sections. The remainder of this walk follows field paths with a short section through Freeholders' Wood.

The climb to the 'summit' of Greets Hill is long and steady along an unfenced moorland road for most of the way – take care walking along the road. Do not explore the old lead mine workings on the flanks of Greets Hill – there are hidden shafts. The moorland sections of this walk are exposed to the elements and may be boggy underfoot, whilst the farmyards may also be muddy. Take particular care when crossing the A684 at Aysgarth Falls and the B6160 at West Burton.

| Ascents: | Greets Hill: | 508 metres |
| | Black Hill (above Apedale): | 420 metres |

Viewpoints:	View from Grinton Moor towards Reeth.
	Superb panorama from Greets Hill.
	Descent towards Castle Bolton.
	Views of Bolton Castle from the path towards Carperby.
	Aysgarth Falls and waterfalls at West Burton.
	View across Bishopdale as you descend towards Eshington Bridge.

FACILITIES

· ·

Reeth	Inn / B&B / Shop / P.O. / Café / Bus / Phone / Toilets / Info. / Camp
Grinton	Inn / B&B / Phone / Bus / Toilets / YH
Castle Bolton	Café / Phone / Bus / Toilets
Carperby	Inn / Bus / Phone
Aysgarth Falls	Inn / B&B / Shop / Café / Bus / Phone / Toilets / Info.
West Burton	Inn / B&B / Shop / P.O. / Café / Bus / Phone

ROUTE DESCRIPTION

· ·

(Map Ten)

Leave Reeth along the 'Richmond' road and follow this road down out of the bottom corner of the large green, then round to reach Reeth Bridge across Arkle Beck. Cross the bridge and follow the road round to the right (with Arkle Beck on your right) then take the FP to the right (SP 'Grinton') just before you enter Fremington. Follow this clear path alongside Arkle Beck passing farm buildings and the remains of Fremington Mill on your left then follow the clear path straight on across the field to join a corner of a stone wall on your left (SP) and follow this round to the left, through a kissing gate then straight on up some steps onto Grinton Bridge across the River Swale. Turn right along the road over the bridge then, where the main road bends sharp left, head straight on along the road (road sign 'Redmire, Leyburn') heading up through Grinton until you reach a cattle grid across the road at the top of the village (unfenced road and open moorland ahead). Take the FP to the right through a small gate immediately before this cattle grid (SP) and follow the unclear FP straight up the heather-covered hillside (no clear path) bearing very slightly to the left until a sharp bend in the unfenced moorland road becomes visible; head up to join the road on this sharp bend (SE 044 974). Follow this unfenced road (Grinton to Redmire road) climbing steadily uphill for approx. 0.75 miles (ignore tracks to your right marked 'Bridleway only - no vehicles) then, where the road levels out, continue along the unfenced road for a further 0.25 miles then, just as the road begins to gently rise up again (stream culvert beneath the road), take the bridleway which branches off to the right away from the road (SP 'bridleway') – *heading towards the two prominent cairns on the summit of Greets Hill in the distance.*

Follow the indistinct grassy path bearing slightly to the right (away from the road) heading across fairly flat moorland at first then rising steadily up across the hillside through an area of old mining spoil heaps (path marked by cairns) up to reach the two prominent cairns on the summit of Greets Hill after 0.75 miles (SE 028 957). Continue along the path passing these cairns to quickly reach a gate in a fence across your path at the top of the hill. Head through the gate then carry straight on to quickly join a clear shooter's track which you follow straight on dropping down into Apedale for approx. 1 mile to reach a junction of tracks at the bottom of the valley (just up from the stone bridge across Apedale Beck and the stone-built shooters' hut). Carry straight on along the stony track down over the bridge across Apedale Beck passing Dent's Houses on your left (stone-built shooters' hut) then continue straight on along the clear track rising steadily up for 0.5 miles to reach a small wall-gate beside a gate in a wall across your path at the top of Black Hill (SE 031 933).

Head through the gate and follow the clear, grassy track straight on (enclosed by fences) then bending down to the right and round to the left (superb views across Wensleydale) then, where the fences end, continue along the grassy track heading straight down across the hillside to reach a wall corner on your right. Carry straight on along the grassy track down alongside the wall on your right, passing a small belt of woodland on your right (Bull Park Plantation) beyond which continue down alongside the wall to soon reach a metal gate set in a wall across your path, just beyond a small bridge across a stream. Head through the gate and follow the enclosed stony track winding down to emerge in Castle Bolton. Turn right along the road across the village green then follow the lane to the right behind Bolton Castle, passing between the Castle and the Church, to reach a gate at the end of the metalled lane (car park on your right). Head through the gate then bear to the left (off the track) across the field (SP 'Aysgarth') to reach a small wall-gate at the bottom end of the wood. Head through the woods to quickly reach another small wall-gate, after which head on bearing slightly to the left down across the field (waymarker posts) and over two stiles across fences, after which head to the right keeping close to the fence and then a stone wall on your right at first (West Bolton Farm ahead) then bear away from the wall slightly down to reach a wall-gate. After the wall-gate drop down over a footbridge across Beldon Beck then bear up to the right and head through a squeeze-stile then walk straight on to reach West Bolton Farm (SE 021 910). Follow the track through the farmyard (keep left of buildings) and take the FP on the right through a small wall-gate immediately after the farm buildings (SP). Head straight on up through another wall-gate, after which continue straight on along the clear path with the wood on your left to reach a bridlegate in a fence at the end of the woods. Continue on down over a small stream then follow the path alongside the stream to reach a wall-gate, after which head straight on keeping close to the fence/wall on your right and through two gates to join a clear (muddy) track that leads to East End Farm. Cross the stile to the left of the gate that leads into the farmyard (muddy) then follow the path to the left of the stone barn to quickly join the road. Turn right along the road into Carperby.

Walk past the Wheatsheaf Hotel, 25 yards after which turn left along a grassy track (SP 'Aysgarth') passing between some houses that quickly leads to a gate on the edge of the village. Head through the gate and walk straight on across the field to soon reach a wall corner protruding slightly into the field. Turn left through a small wall-gate in this wall corner (SP) then walk straight across the field alongside the wall on your left to quickly reach a squeeze-stile in a wall across your path – do not head through this but turn right (SP 'Aysgarth') and head down across two fields, keeping close to the wall on your left, to reach a squeeze-stile that leads onto a narrow walled lane (Low Lane). At the lane, take the FP opposite to the right through a squeeze-stile (SP 'Aysgarth') then, after about 150 yards, head right through a squeeze-stile (SP) after which continue on along the clear path bearing to the right across the middle of the field, through a wall-gate then carry on through two more squeeze-stiles to reach Freeholders Wood. As you enter the wood, follow the clear path to the right meandering through the woods to reach the road. Turn left along the road then right just after the railway bridge up into the Yorkshire Dales National Park Information Centre car park. Walk straight on across the car park (passing the Information Centre on your left) to join a path at the far end, which you follow down to the left to reach the road at Yore Bridge above Aysgarth Falls (Upper Falls). Cross Yore Bridge then, as the road bends to the right, head straight on up the steps between Yore Mill and the cottages and through the churchyard to reach St Andrew's Church. Pass the church on your left and continue straight on up through the churchyard then along an enclosed path to reach the main road (A684) - SE 013 883.

Cross the road *(take care)* and take the FP directly opposite (SP 'Eshington Bridge') and follow the clear path straight on through a small wall-gate then steeply down into a dip, over a stile (SP) then up to reach another wall-gate. After this wall-gate, head on alongside the stone wall on your left over the brow of the hill (SP) then bear away from the wall to the right through a small gate in a fence. Continue straight on bearing to the left down across the hillside, through a wall-gate (in a section of stone wall) then on to quickly reach another wall-gate after which head straight down the field through a wall-gate beside a large tree (to the left of a gate) that leads onto the road near Eshington Bridge (SE 015 878). Turn right along the road over Eshington Bridge, just after which take the FP to the right (SP 'West Burton') and head straight on across the field to reach a stile. After the stile follow the clear path (Bishopdale Beck across to your right) straight on across the field alongside the wall on your right then, where this wall bends away, continue straight on along the clear path to reach a squeeze-stile to your left in the corner of the field beside a bend in the river (Bishopdale Beck). After this squeeze-stile, head straight on (Bishopdale Beck on your right) to quickly reach another squeeze-stile then head straight on (away from the river) across the field passing through a gateway to the right of a barn then straight on across the next field to reach a stile by a gate that leads onto the road. Cross the road *(take care)* and head up the steps opposite to the right (SP 'West Burton') and follow the path up between the houses to join a road at West Burton, where you turn right up to reach the green in the centre of the village (SE 017 867).

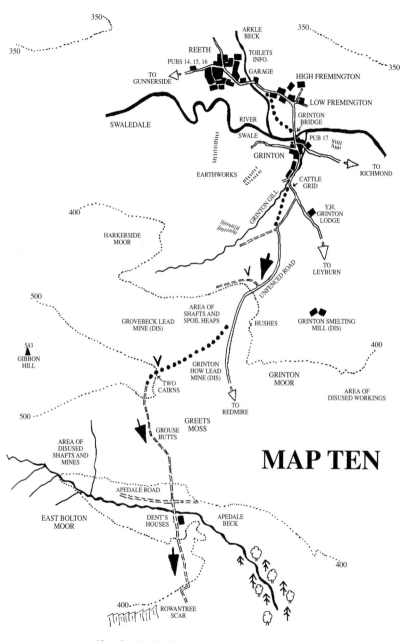

REETH

ARKLE BECK

TOILETS INFO.

PUBS 14, 15, 16

GARAGE

TO GUNNERSIDE

HIGH FREMINGTON

LOW FREMINGTON

SWALEDALE

RIVER

SWALE

GRINTON BRIDGE

PUB 17

GRINTON

TO RICHMOND

EARTHWORKS

CATTLE GRID

GRINTON GILL

Y.H. GRINTON LODGE

350

350

350

350

400

HARKERSIDE MOOR

UNFENCED ROAD

TO LEYBURN

500

AREA OF SHAFTS AND SPOIL HEAPS

GROVEBECK LEAD MINE (DIS)

HUSHES

GRINTON SMELTING MILL (DIS)

400

543 GIBBON HILL

TWO CAIRNS

GRINTON HOW LEAD MINE (DIS)

GRINTON MOOR

AREA OF DISUSED WORKINGS

500

TO REDMIRE

GREETS MOSS

GROUSE BUTTS

MAP TEN

AREA OF DISUSED SHAFTS AND MINES

APEDALE ROAD

EAST BOLTON MOOR

DENT'S HOUSES

APEDALE BECK

400

400

ROWANTREE SCAR

©Crown Copyright 2005. All rights reserved. Licence Number 100011978

MAP ELEVEN

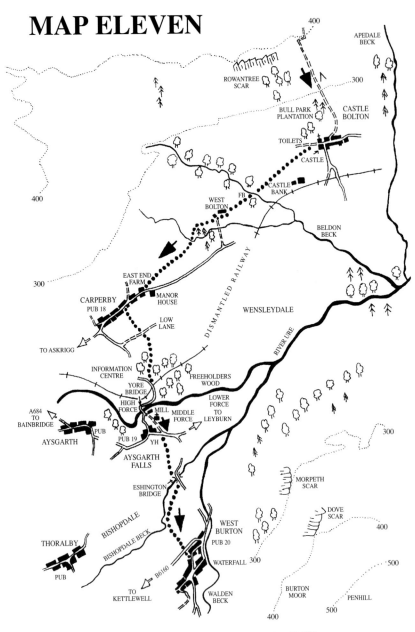

400

APEDALE BECK

ROWANTREE SCAR

300

BULL PARK PLANTATION

CASTLE BOLTON

TOILETS

CASTLE

CASTLE BANK

WEST BOLTON

FB

BELDON BECK

400

300

EAST END FARM

MANOR HOUSE

CARPERBY
PUB 18

LOW LANE

WENSLEYDALE

DISMANTLED RAILWAY

RIVER URE

TO ASKRIGG

INFORMATION CENTRE

YORE BRIDGE

FREEHOLDERS WOOD

HIGH FORCE

MILL

MIDDLE FORCE

LOWER FORCE TO LEYBURN

A684 TO BAINBRIDGE

PUB

300

AYSGARTH

PUB 19

YH

AYSGARTH FALLS

ESHINGTON BRIDGE

BISHOPDALE

BISHOPDALE BECK

WEST BURTON

PUB 20

MORPETH SCAR

DOVE SCAR

400

THORALBY

WATERFALL

300

500

PUB

B6160

BURTON MOOR

PENHILL

TO KETTLEWELL

WALDEN BECK

400

500

©Crown Copyright 2005. All rights reserved. Licence Number 100011978

GRINTON is a jumble of pretty stone cottages, a sturdy bridge over the Swale, a lovely old pub and St Andrew's Church, the 'Cathedral of the Dales'. This site has been a place of worship since pre-conquest days, originally for pagan ceremonies later being adopted by the Christian church, however, the first church was built during Norman times. Fragments of the Norman church survive today in the form of part of the chancel arch, a small window and the bowl of the font. The present church dates largely from the 14th to 16th Centuries and was built by the monks of Bridlington Priory, although restoration of the building took place in 1896. It is the quintessential Dales church - a long and low stone building with a squat bell tower that seems to blend in perfectly with its surroundings. Up until Tudor times St Andrew's Church served the whole of Swaledale stretching up to the old Westmorland border, which made it one of the largest parishes in the country. This was the only consecrated ground in Swaledale which meant that the dead had to be carried in wicker baskets for the 12 mile journey from the dale head to the church along the 'Corpse Way'; thankfully a church was built in Muker at 1580. In the 17th Century a law was passed to help the declining woollen trade whereby the dead had to be buried in a woollen shroud. Adam Barker, a local man, made the mistake of burying his daughter in a linen shroud in the churchyard at Grinton in 1692 and was subsequently fined £5. As a focal point for such a large catchment area Grinton became an important meeting place, weekly Sunday markets were held here for the benefit of the worshippers despite the fact that the medieval church poured scorn on such non-religious events, especially on a Sunday. Today the church is a place of eternal peace, *"A heavy border of yews running round the churchyard.....seem to gather round as if to protect the church from the storms which sweep down the dale. There is a feeling of age and history in the burial ground; it has gathered to itself from the bounds of a great parish so many sons and daughters of the dale. The grey church tower seems to call its children, the wide aisles on either side to stretch out sheltering arms, and the battlemented clerestory behind to offer security. The church gazes up the dale as it did long centuries ago, watching for those slow processions down the old corpse way."* (**E. Pontefract & M. Hartley 'Swaledale' 1934**). It is worth exploring the church as it boasts many interesting features, such as the 'Lepers Squint' which allowed lepers to watch the service from outside the nave, a chained copy of Birkett's New Testament on a 14th Century stand, ancient stained glass and grooves in the stonework by the porch where arrows were sharpened by men waiting for their lords who were attending a pre-hunt service!

Perched on Grinton Moor near to the Leyburn road is Grinton Lodge. This 19th Century battlemented building was once the shooting lodge of Colonel Charlesworth, however, it has been a Youth Hostel since the 1940s. This area also affords some of the best views in Swaledale including a wonderful view back towards Reeth with its large sloping green set on the lower flanks of Calver Hill looking out across the wide confluence of the River Swale and Arkle Beck with the gleaming limestone scars of Fremington Edge towering above. *"....the green valley of Arkengarthdale stretches out like a promised land; and there is a glimpse of Swaledale, winding round to the left, just enough to set you longing for its upland regions."* (**E. Pontefract & M. Hartley 1934**).

GREETS HILL is actually an undulation along a broad and gently rising ridge of moorland that stretches for several miles forming the watershed between Swaledale and Wensleydale, rising to a maximum height of 555 metres above sea level on the 'summit' of High Carl at the head of Apedale. Greets Hill, along with neighbouring Coal Pit Moor and Grinton Moor, is scarred with old mine workings, spoil heaps and bell pits. These bell pits, so called because they look like inverted bells, were the earliest form of lead extraction that date back to between the 16th and 18th Centuries, although some date back to medieval times. Miners would find a seam of lead ore and then dig down to extract the mineral-bearing rock, piling the debris around the opening of the shallow, vertical pit. These bell pits often follow straight lines across the moors as miners followed the mineral veins. Poor quality coal was also dug out from these moorland heights and was used to fire the hearths of the smelt mills, as well as for domestic fires. As technology advanced during the

18th Century these bell pits were gradually replaced by levels driven horizontally into the hillside along a vein, with vertical shafts connecting various veins and minefields. A glance at the map reveals dozens of hushes, abandoned workings, spoil heaps and shafts scattered across this moorland, including Grinton Lead Smelt Mill hidden away in Cogden Gill, the best preserved lead smelt mill in the Yorkshire Dales. This smelt mill dates from around 1820, although a smelt mill has stood on the site since the early 18th Century, and was in use up until 1895 when the company went bankrupt.

Greets Hill is the highest ground between the Yorkshire Dales and North York Moor and as such provides a vast panorama with Teesside clearly visible on the horizon, whilst to the south lies Wensleydale with Great Whernside and Buckden Pike rising above.

APEDALE was once a major centre for lead mining in Wensleydale, which has left a legacy of spoil heaps, mine shafts and miles of glorious green lanes and gravel tracks. It is a lonely, desolate and relatively unknown valley hidden away amongst the hills between Swaledale and Wensleydale, whose only occupants are sheep, rabbits and grouse (unfortunately no monkeys!). However, if you enjoy wild places then you will fall in love with the haunting beauty of Apedale. Its unusual name is not derived from apes but from the personal name 'Appi', a Viking chieftain who settled here over 1,000 years ago, although the moorland that rises to over 540 metres at the head of Apedale is known as Gibbon Hill – perhaps there are some of our hairy relatives here after all! *"A moor often has the desolation of death about it, but it teems with life. Put your back against it, and look at the sky, and listen. Listen carefully. Out of the profound stillness comes a magnitude of tiny sounds. There are marching armies in the grass, winged battalions hovering above it. I have seen some fine dramas played amongst the tangled roots of heather. Sudden slaughter, terror, love, hate and passion: all the elements of first class drama are presented here. The actors are lilliputian; the stage may be a blade of grass, or the petal of a mountain pansy. But the events you witness are grim; the players are in earnest. Feeling runs pretty high even among crawling pinheads. Next time you have an idle day, make yourself a couch on a quiet moor, and lie down.*

Sleep, if you are tired. But first, for a while, listen. And learn." (**A. Wainwright 'A Pennine Journey - The Story of a Long Walk in 1938' 1986**). The descent from Apedale towards Castle Bolton affords superb views across Wensleydale above the ramparts of the castle towards Penhill, Walden, Bishopdale and Addlebrough – a strategic spot indeed.

CASTLE BOLTON, with its old stone cottages lining the green, is completely dwarfed by the majestic Bolton Castle. The castle was built in 1399 by Richard le Scrope, the Chancellor of England to Richard II, and took 18 years to complete at a cost of £12,000, an incredible sum of money in those days. Its walls are nine feet thick and stand 130 feet wide by 180 feet long, with four massive corner towers nearly 100 feet high enclosing a central courtyard. It was designed more as a fortified house with comfort in mind than a defensive castle. *"Lord Scrope, High Chancellor of England, obtained King Richard's licence to fortify his manorial residence at Bolton, in the third year of his reign; and eighteen changeful years swept past before the lordly pile was completed at a cost of 18,000 marks. Patient oxen drew the necessary wood from Engleby Forest, in Cumberland, and the masonary of the castle was calculated to withstand leaguer and storm, should evil days of internecine strife trouble the nation."* (**W. Andrews 'Bygone Yorkshire' 1892**). Many of the galleries and great halls are still supported by these 600 year old oak beams. The stone for the castle came from quarries in Apedale and local legend also tells us that these early builders used ox blood mixed with the mortar to give it added strength. *"...it had chimneys - at that time revolutionary features in England."* (**M. Hartley & J. Ingilby 'The Wonders of Yorkshire' 1959**). The castle occupies a commanding position and dominates much of Wensleydale; it can be seen for miles around, *"....but to me the appeal of the castle is in its situation - all-seeing and visible from such great distances, dwarfing its surroundings."* (**J. Herriot 'James Herriot's Yorkshire' 1979**).

The castle has witnessed a number of pivotal moments in English history. *"The wind sighed through the ruins with a wailing, melancholy sound; dark patches of storm clouds were swiftly sailing across the heavens, hiding the full-orbed queen of the night, and casting dense shadows on the old fortress, which presented a stern, gloomy, and desolate look almost awe-inspiring. Now and again for a brief few moments the moon rode from behind the jagged clouds, shedding forth, on the stern and silent castle, rays of subdued splendour. As we stood gazing on the mighty structure, with not a sound to disturb our reverie, save that caused by the flight of a solitary night bird, and the wind rustling amongst the ivy and shivering of withered leaves, bygone scenes and actors in life's great drama flit in imagination before our gaze."* (**E. Bogg 'From Eden Vale to the Plains of York'**). Mary, Queen of Scots was imprisoned in the castle from July 1568 until January 1569 before being taken to Tutbury Castle in Staffordshire. She was treated well during her stay at Bolton Castle, having her own chambers and forty servants, although legend has it that she attempted to escape but was recaptured on Leyburn Shawl at a spot that is now known as 'The Queen's Gap'. The castle played an important role in the English Civil war as a garrison for Royalist forces, however Parliamentary forces besieged the castle in 1645 and the Royalists surrendered. The castle was made untenable in 1647, under orders from Cromwell, after which it remained uninhabited for almost three centuries; the weakening of the structure in 1647 contributed to the collapse of the north east tower during a storm in 1761. *"In the battle of Flodden, which ended in a victory for England, the lusty lads of Wensleydale were in the thick of the fight."* (**W. Andrews**

'Picturesque Yorkshire'). The 11th Lord Scrope died in 1636 after which the estate passed to his illegitimate son John, who defended Bolton Castle for the King during the Civil War. John died of the plague soon after surrendering and the estate passed to his sister Mary who married Charles Powlett in 1653, who later became the Duke of Bolton. Further down the dale, near to Wensley, stands Bolton Hall which was built in 1678 by the fourth Duke of Bolton as the family home instead of the ruinous castle; the castle and hall are still owned and occupied by Lord Bolton. I recommend a tour of the castle to see the great halls, chapel, armoury, kitchens and dungeons carved out of solid rock where an arm bone was found still manacled to the dungeon wall.

To the north of the castle stands St Oswald's Church which was built in 1325, pre-dating the castle by almost 70 years. Note the grooves in the stonework beside the door caused by the sharpening of arrows and swords, a reminder of less peaceful times. *"In another position the little church of St Oswald would be a normal size for the village, but, standing close under the castle walls, it seems a toy building, and for most of the day the sun is hidden from it....Probably one of the last instances of public apology took place here. A woman had slandered another, and the apology was demanded by the whole village. During the service she had to walk up and down the aisle, and at the end of it make her apology, which she did in rhyme."* **(E. Pontefract & M. Hartley 'Wensleydale' 1936).** Close by is the old village post office which makes a perfect 'chocolate box' picture.

CARPERBY is an ancient village which was mentioned in the Domesday Book, when it was known as 'Kerparbi', and has had long traditions of farming and trading. The Wensleydale breed of sheep were reputedly first recognised and named here in the late 19th Century. This rare breed is the largest and heaviest of all sheep breeds and is noted for its coat of long ringlets of fine wool. The village was granted a market charter in 1305, one of the earliest markets in the Yorkshire Dales, although by the 16th Century the weekly markets had lapsed in favour of nearby Askrigg. There is a fine stepped market cross in the centre of the village dated 1674, complete with some very unusual carved faces in the stonework; the date of this market cross probably comes from when the old cross was restored. Superbly preserved medieval cultivation terraces, or lynchets, can be found in the fields behind the village from days when crops were grown in the dale, hence the name of the pub. The 'Wheatsheaf Hotel' was the honeymoon hotel of the real life James Herriot in 1941. *"Our bedroom, with its brass bedstead, looked out over the old roofs of the village across the Ure to the hills beyond, and I still feel that wherever Helen and I might have spent our honeymoon we could not have found greater beauty."* (**J. Herriot 1979**). The impressive Friends' Meeting House dated 1864 indicates the importance of Quakerism in this area. Today, Carperby is a quiet place with quaint stone cottages lining the road which runs through the village.

FREEHOLDERS' WOOD is a remnant of the ancient woodland that once covered much of Wensleydale. A wide variety of deciduous species can be found here including elm, oak, ash, rowan, birch, wild cherry, holly and hazel covering an area of thirty-two acres beside Aysgarth Falls. For centuries this wood has been managed on a rotational coppicing basis where trees are cut back to ground level, new shoots are allowed to grow to a usable thickness and then they are harvested; the villagers of Carperby still have rights to gather wood, hence its name of Freeholders' Wood. It is now owned and managed by the Yorkshire Dales National Park who bought it from the Bolton Estate over ten years ago. The wood had been neglected and allowed to grow wild, but they have re-introduced coppicing which has benefited the fauna and flora of the wood. The woodland is noted for its wild flowers in spring, as well as birds such as chaffinch, treecreeper, goldcrest and bullfinch as well as mammals such as roe deer and, very rarely, red squirrels. The successful management of Freeholders' Wood has led to the Forestry Commission declaring it a woodland centre of excellence. Paths through the wood lead to the Middle and Lower Falls of the world-renowned Aysgarth Falls. *"The trees make an archway over the path which leads to the Lower Falls, whose roaring when the river is in flood is heard like thunder long before they are reached. The volume of water tossing and swirling is impressive, though there is terror in its fascination, but these falls are beautiful at all times.*

With the sound of them in your ears you return along the path. Dusk falls, and the gloom of the wood is intensified. For you the road lies just beyond, but you realize here the difficulties of those early travellers in the forest, and their terror when night was coming on, of being lost." (**E. Pontefract & M. Hartley 1936**).

THE WENSLEYDALE RAILWAY once connected the Settle to Carlisle line at Garsdale Head with the main North East line at Northallerton. Work began on the Wensleydale Railway in 1848, although it took a full thirty years to complete the line in its entirety. The railway from Northallerton to Hawes was actually built by the North Eastern Railway, who operated the East Coast Mainline, whilst the line from Hawes to Garsdale Head was built by the Midland Railway Company to link up with their Settle to Carlisle Railway. This railway provided a vital link across the heart of England for almost a century, bringing a pulse of life to remote communities as well as offering one of the most scenic journeys in the country with the railway line snaking its way up through the spectacular landscape of Wensleydale. Sadly, the railway closed for passengers in 1954 and freight in 1964, although the tracks were kept between Northallerton and Redmire to service the nearby limestone quarries and, more recently, to transport M.O.D. equipment to the ranges above Wensleydale.

The Wensleydale Railway Association was formed in 1990 with the aim of re-establishing the link to Garsdale Head and resume passenger services along the remaining track-bed between Northallerton and Redmire; that momentous day came on July 4th 2003 with the first regular passenger service for almost 50 years between Leeming Bar and Leyburn. In 2004, three more stations were re-opened at Redmire, Finghall and Bedale. There are plans to extend passenger services to Northallerton to connect with the East Coast Mainline whilst the ultimate goal is to restore the entire 40-mile route from Northallerton to Garsdale Head.

AYSGARTH FALLS make up one of the tourist 'honey-pots' of the Yorkshire Dales, and it easy to understand why. *"Ah, exquisite*

Aysgarth! Who would not strive and strive again to reach some true expression of the fair picture which lies glowing in his memory! Words are but a palisade, through whose chinks one can, at most, catch some gleam of all that beauty, and while I sit and vainly steep my senses in the roar and turmoil of the flashing water, I know well that I might as easily describe a swallow's flight as the abounding loveliness of this great fall at Aysgarth." (A. Norway 'Highways and Byways in Yorkshire' 1899). The River Ure tumbles over rock terraces in a series of waterfalls which stretch for over a mile through a beautiful narrow wooded valley, dropping over 200 feet along the way. There are three groupings of falls; the Upper Falls have the most attractive setting and are best viewed from Yore Bridge, however, the Middle and Lower Falls are the most spectacular, especially after heavy rain, and can be reached by following the clearly marked paths through Freeholders' Wood. *"It is stirring to come here after a storm and see the River Ure roaring along its stony bed under the trees. Rushing impetuously in a flood hemmed in by limestone walls and overhanging woods, tumbling down rocky ledges like the steps of a giant's staircase, the water breaks into amber foam; and the roar of the river can be heard like the thunder of a thousand horses on Leyburn Shawl six miles away. It was a spectacle that enchanted Turner, and is one of the finest sights in the Dales, which must be seen for its enthralling beauty to be believed."* (A. Mee 'Yorkshire North Riding' 1941).

Next to Yore Bridge, which originally dates from the late 16th Century and widened in 1788, stands Yore Mill. This mill was built in 1784 and stands as a wonderful example of an early water-powered mill complex set magnificently beside the powerful River Ure. The mill was destroyed by fire and rebuilt in the 1850s, and has been used as a flour, wool and cotton mill over the years; the famous red shirts for Garibaldi's army came from here! The mill ceased production in the 1950s and now houses a craft shop and tea rooms.

ST ANDREW'S CHURCH dates mainly from 1866 when rebuilding work took place; some remnants of the original late 12th Century church remain in the lower part of the tower. St Andrew's was, for many centuries, the main church in upper Wensleydale and has the largest churchyard in the country. The Aysgarth parish once stretched for 81,000 acres, although this has now been sub-divided. *"There is about Aysgarth church some feeling of its old importance and domination. It had control over the churches higher up the dale, churches much poorer than itself, a position which its vicars sometimes exploited to their own advantage."* (**E. Pontefract & M. Hartley 1936**). Inside the church there is a beautifully carved wooden screen and a reading desk made from two carved bench ends bearing the 'Rebus' of William de Heslington, Abbot of Jervaulx from 1472. These were carved by the famous Ripon Carvers in about 1506 and were originally housed at Jervaulx Abbey, coming to Aysgarth at the Dissolution of the Monasteries. There is an oak beam in the chancel with unusual carvings and the initials of the last Abbot of Jervaulx, Adam Sedbergh dated 1536. Close by is the curiously named Palmer Flatt Hotel, whose unusual name is a reminder of monastic days; the hotel stands on the site of a medieval hospice for pilgrims.

BISHOPDALE, Wensleydale's largest tributary, is well-known to many visitors because the main connecting road between Wharfedale and Wensleydale travels through the valley. The dale stretches six miles from the wild upper reaches at Kidstones Pass to the more placid surroundings at Aysgarth. After the last Ice Age Bishopdale was filled by a glacial lake which deposited silts on the land, thus giving the valley floor particularly fertile soils. *"The soil of Bishopdale produces the richest grass in the county, in some instances the land has let at £5 per acre."* (**E. Bogg**). This fertile land has helped give Bishopdale a long and successful history of hunting and farming. During the Middle Ages the dale was the hunting preserve of the noblemen of Middleham Castle, who travelled to this valley via the old track of Morpeth Gate that cuts a high-level course across the northern flanks of Penhill. Their ownership ended in the 17th Century which gave the tenant farmers an opportunity to buy holdings and build their own houses; Bishopdale has some of the best examples of 17th Century yeoman long-houses in the Yorkshire Dales which are characterised by mullioned windows and carved door lintels. *"Here, scattered about the fell-sides and in the valley, are some of the finest and oldest of those stone* *built farmsteads for which the North-West Riding is so noted. Many of them are of great antiquity; some have histories attaching to them. At Thoralby, one of the most ancient villages hereabouts, the parish records of which go back to pre-Norman times, there is a farmstead which was originally a hunting-lodge of the great Barons of Rokeby."* (**Fletcher 'Nooks and Corners of Yorkshire').**

WEST BURTON is one of the loveliest villages in the Yorkshire Dales, indeed some claim it to be the most beautiful village in England and it is easy to see why. It is situated on the flanks of Naughtberry Hill, which divides Walden valley from Bishopdale, and is a peaceful almost secret place. This is because the main Bishopdale road by-passes the village and the road through the village and up into the Walden valley is a no-through route. The village has an idyllic setting; wooded hills look down upon a surprisingly large village green, complete with stocks and a stone stepped obelisk that dates from 1820, surrounded by ancient stone cottages. This obelisk is not a market cross as West Burton has never had a market, nor has it ever had a church, hence the number of footpaths that lead from the villages of Bishopdale to St Andrew's Church at Aysgarth Falls. *"But perhaps West Burton, at the foot of Waldendale, is the gem of all in Wensleydale, with school, stocks, and cross alongside the green, and the parish corn mill grinding away at the bottom next to the stream."* (**W. T. Palmer 'Odd corners in the Yorkshire Dales' 1937**). The Fox and Hounds overlooks the green and is a typical Dales village pub; functional yet comfortable with excellent local ale; to sit outside this pub on a warm summer's evening enjoying a glass of beer surrounded by such wonderful scenery is an experience not to be missed. In the 19th Century there was another pub in the village called the Black Bull Inn, which occupied the house that stands in the middle of the village green just beyond the obelisk. Despite the closure of this pub long ago, village life continues to flourish with a well-stocked shop and Post Office, tea rooms, pub, primary school, butcher's shop and craft workshops.

Out of the bottom corner of the green, a track leads down past the old mill to reach West Burton Falls, also known as Cauldron Force, which has a delightful setting amongst rocks and overhanging trees where the waters of Walden Beck cascade over rock ledges into a deep pool. *"It was early autumn on our visit, and the branches of the trees and pale golden leaves were drooping feather-like over the rocks, outlined against the blue sky; through this leafy screen the crystal waters can be seen flowing towards the deep limestone scarr, over which it leaps with tumultuous sound, then whirling into eddies and a series of small falls, darts under the most picturesque of bridges thrown here and there across its waters, and as it courses along in merry career, past the creamy walls of Burton, carrying on its bosom the crisp autumn leaves, the overhanging trees stoop, as it were, to be kissed and reflected in the beautiful waters."* (**E. Bogg**). The track which crosses Walden Beck near to the waterfall by way of a packhorse bridge forms part of the ancient packhorse route from West Burton to Middleham, known as Morpeth Gate. This old road, now a stony track, was once a busy route between West Burton and the important market town of Middleham, with its historic castle. It is possible that this was originally a Roman road from the fort at Bainbridge, later used by the Lords of Middleham Castle as a quick route to their hunting forest in Bishopdale.

WEST BURTON
to
KETTLEWELL

✦

*"After visiting the isolated farm, I couldn't resist pulling my car off the unfenced
road and climbing with my beagle, Dinah, to the high country which beckoned
me. The snow had disappeared almost overnight leaving only runnels of white
lying behind the walls and it was as though all the scents of the earth and
growing things had been imprisoned and were released now by the spring
sunshine in waves of piercing sweetness. When I reached the summit I was
breathless and gulped the crystal air greedily as though I could never get enough
of it. Here there was no evidence of the hand of man and I walked with
my dog among miles of heather, peat hags and bog pools with the black waters
rippling and the tufts of rushes bending and swaying in the eternal wind.
As the cloud shadows, racing on the wind, flew over me, trailing ribbons of
shade and brightness over the endless browns and greens, I felt a rising
exhilaration at being up there on the roof of Yorkshire. It was an empty
landscape where no creature stirred and it was silent except for the cry of a
distant bird, yet I felt a further surge of excitement in the solitude, a tingling
sense of the nearness of all creation."*

J. Herriot
'Every Living Thing' 1992.

WALK INFORMATION

Points of interest: The 'secret' valley of the Welsh, monastic and stagecoach routes, a remote Dales' inn, wonderful river scenery, stones with strange powers, Brigantes dikes, wild desolate moorland and a bird's eye view of Wharfedale.

Distance:

West Burton to Horsehouse	5 miles
Horsehouse to Kettlewell	9 miles
Total	14 miles

Time: Allow 7 hours

Terrain: Most of this walk either follows unfenced surfaced roads or clear gravel/turf bridleways. The sections between West Burton and Cote Bridge as well as Horsehouse and Woodale follow riverside paths across meadowland. The climb from Woodale to the head of Coverdale is long and steady, whilst the final descent into Kettlewell follows a rough and rocky track (Top Mere Road) that is steep in places. Excellent walking terrain all the way.

Take care walking along the roads through Walden and Coverdale. This walk includes two climbs up onto Fleensop Moor and Great Hunters Sleets at the head of Coverdale, whilst the descent into Wharfedale follows a rough, steep track. Fleensop Moor and Great Hunters Sleets are exposed to the elements.

Ascents:

Fleensop Moor:	445 metres
Top Mere Gate:	530 metres

Viewpoints: View from Fleensop Moor across Walden Valley. Descent towards Horsehouse with views across Coverdale.

River scenery through Coverdale.

View down Wharfedale from Great Hunters Sleets (Tor Dike).

View down Wharfedale across the rooftops of Kettlewell from Top Mere Road.

FACILITIES

West Burton	Inn / B&B / Shop / P.O. / Café / Bus / Phone
Horsehouse	Inn / B&B / Phone / Camp
Woodale	B&B
Kettlewell	Inn / B&B / Shop / P.O. / Café / Bus / Phone / Toilets / YH / Camp

ROUTE DESCRIPTION

(Map Twelve)

From the centre of West Burton, walk up across the village green then, just after the stone-built obelisk and house in the middle of the green, take the road-turning to the left (road sign 'Walden only'). Follow this quiet lane gently rising up out of the village for 0.25 miles then, where fields open out on your left, take the FP to the left (SP 'Rookwith bridge, Cote Bridge'). Bear to the right across the field then drop down to the left to reach Rookwith Bridge (FB) across Walden Beck, immediately after which turn right through a squeeze-stile (SP 'Cote Bridge'). Head straight on across the field, keeping close to the field perimeter and river on your right, to reach a gate just to the right of a small barn that leads onto an enclosed track which you follow straight on to reach the road beside Cote Bridge. Turn left and follow the metalled road heading steadily up through the Walden valley passing the turning for Whiterow Farm on your right after 1 mile where you continue along the road bending sharply up to the left to reach a cattle grid across the road at the top of this hill (road levels out) just after which take the stony track to the left (SE 017 837). Follow this clear stony track up through a gate then bending to the right climbing steadily up across the hillside then turning sharply up to the left (at an old railway carriage) to reach a gate in a wall at the top of the climb. After the gate, head straight on along the stony track which soon comes to an end – carry straight on along the rough grassy path heading across the top of the open moorland (White Hill) for 0.3 miles to reach another gate in a wall.

Head through this gate and follow the clear track to the right alongside the wall at first then bearing to the left across the open moorland of Fleensop Moor gently dropping down to reach a fork in the track beside some grouse butts. Continue straight on bearing slightly to the right passing between the grouse butts (SP) then on passing the turning to the left towards Fleensop Farm *(with the small valley of Fleemis Gill stretching away to your left)* – continue straight on along the clear stony track and follow this through a gate in a wall then down to reach a ford across Fleemis Gill (above a small rocky ravine). After the ford, continue along the stony track heading up across the hillside for 0.3 miles until the track joins a stone wall on your left where you head through the gate in this wall – do not continue up along the stony track (SE 027 814). After the gate, follow the rough grassy path bearing gradually to the right up across the moorland (Fleemis Gill falling away down to your left) until it joins a stone wall on your right – head through the small wooden gate in this wall. After the wall-gate, head diagonally to the left down across the field along a narrow path to reach a gate in the bottom left-hand corner, after which continue straight on for a short distance to reach a stone wall across your path. Turn right and follow the clear (eroded) path down the hillside alongside this wall to reach a ladder stile beside a gate at the top of an enclosed track – follow this enclosed stony track down to reach the road at Horsehouse (SE 047 813).

(Map Thirteen)

Turn right along the road, past the Thwaite Arms and out of the village. Continue along the road for 0.25 miles then take the road turning to the left towards 'Arkleside only', down over Arkleside

Bridge after which follow the road to the right alongside the River Cover to soon reach another stone bridge across a side-stream (Arkleside Gill). Immediately after this bridge take the FP to the right through the gate (SP 'Woodale') and head straight on across the field then, halfway across the field (SP), bear to the left to reach a small wall-gap that leads onto a farm track (just beyond the houses of Arkleside). Turn right along this lane (ignore the track up to the left) and follow this straight on then, where this lane turns to the right towards a stone farmhouse, carry straight on through a gate along a grassy track to reach another gate to the right of a small barn at the end of the track. Head through this gate and walk across the field keeping close to the field perimeter on your left to reach a stile in the top left corner of the field, after which bear up to the right to quickly reach a FB across Harkera Gill. Cross the FB and up some steps to a stile, after which carry straight on alongside the wall on your right for a short distance then turn right over a wall stile (SP 'Braidley') and drop down to reach a large FB across the River Cover (SE 037 799).

Turn left immediately after the FB across the River Cover and follow the riverside path straight on to quickly reach a gate in a wall across your path, after which follow the rough grassy track straight on heading up the valley with the river just to your left (ignore the track up towards Braidley) to reach a gate across your path beside a stone barn (where the rough track bends to the left and fords the river). Head through this gate and carry straight on (still with the river to your left) across a number of fields through a series of wall-gaps/gates to re-emerge on the riverside path where you continue straight on alongside the stone wall on your right. As you approach the houses of Woodale just up to your right, cross over the small side-stream of Fall Gill just after which head through the gate in the wall corner on your right and follow the track up through the farmyard to reach the road at Woodale. Turn left along the road and follow it climbing up out of Woodale then levelling out for 0.5 miles before bending steeply down to reach Cover Bridge beside the entrance to Coverhead Farm.

Cross Cover Bridge and continue along the road climbing quite steeply at first then more gradually (with lots of dips and small turns) for a further 1.25 miles heading up into the upper reaches of Coverdale (unfenced road for much of the way) before the road bends steeply up to the left to reach Hunter's Stone (prominent slender stone) beside the road. The unfenced road levels out slightly and gently rises up to reach a cattle grid, after which continue on for a further 0.25 miles across the top of the 'pass' (summit ridge of Great Whernside up to your left) then take the grassy track that branches off to the right (SP 'Starbotton, Kettlewell') - SD 989 762. Follow this clear grassy track gradually bearing away from the road heading across the open moorland of Great Hunters Sleets. After a while, the grassy track curves to the right (another track joins it from the left) then runs alongside a stone wall (Tor Dike on the other side of the wall) to reach a gate/stile in a wall corner. Head through the gate and continue on along the clear, undulating rough path alongside the wall on your left skirting around the head of the valley, through another gate (Top Mere Gate) and carry straight on (wall bends away to the left) to reach a fork in the track (junction of Starbotton Road with Top Mere Road). At this junction, bear left (SP 'Kettlewell') and follow the clear track gently dropping down across the open moorland of Cam Head to reach a gate across your path after approx. 0.5 miles (SD 970 747). Continue straight on along the clear grassy track heading down across the grassy moorland (Wharfedale in the distance). The track soon becomes a walled stony lane known as Top Mere Road that leads steeply down (superb views of Wharfedale) for just over 1 mile to eventually join the metalled road on a sharp bend just above Kettlewell. Follow this road straight on steeply down into Kettlewell village (SD 972 725).

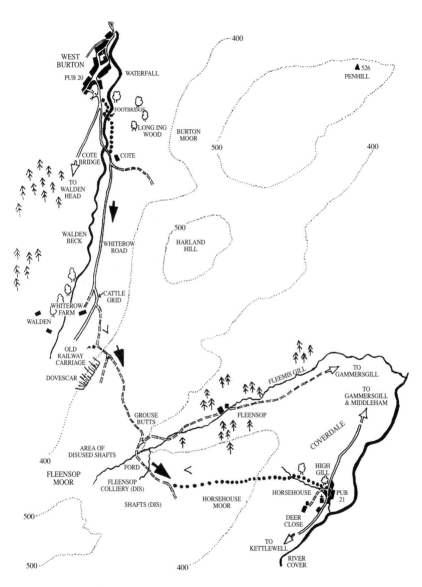

WEST
BURTON

PUB 20   WATERFALL

400

▲ 526
PENHILL

FOOTBRIDGE

LONG ING
WOOD

BURTON
MOOR

COTE
BRIDGE   COTE

500

400

TO
WALDEN
HEAD

WALDEN
BECK   WHITEROW
ROAD

500

HARLAND
HILL

CATTLE
GRID

WHITEROW
FARM

WALDEN

OLD
RAILWAY
CARRIAGE

DOVESCAR

FLEEMIS GILL

TO
GAMMERSGILL

TO
GAMMERSGILL
& MIDDLEHAM

GROUSE
BUTTS

FLEENSOP

COVERDALE

AREA OF
DISUSED SHAFTS

400

FLEENSOP
MOOR

FORD

FLEENSOP
COLLIERY (DIS)

HIGH
GILL

HORSEHOUSE

PUB
21

SHAFTS (DIS)

HORSEHOUSE
MOOR

DEER
CLOSE

500

TO
KETTLEWELL

500

400

RIVER
COVER

MAP TWELVE

©Crown Copyright 2005. All rights reserved. Licence Number 100011978

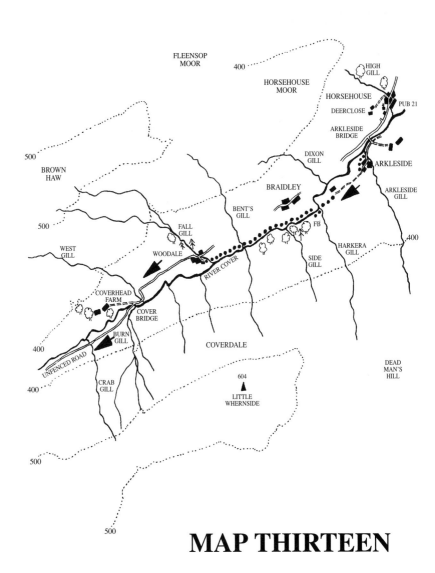

FLEENSOP
MOOR
400

HIGH
GILL

HORSEHOUSE
MOOR

HORSEHOUSE

PUB 21

DEERCLOSE

ARKLESIDE
BRIDGE

DIXON
GILL

ARKLESIDE

500

BROWN
HAW

ARKLESIDE
GILL

BRAIDLEY

BENT'S
GILL

500

FALL
GILL

FB

WEST
GILL

HARKERA
GILL

400

WOODALE

RIVER COVER

SIDE
GILL

COVERHEAD
FARM

COVER
BRIDGE

BURN
GILL

400

COVERDALE

DEAD
MAN'S
HILL

UNFENCED ROAD

CRAB
GILL

604

400

LITTLE
WHERNSIDE

500

500

MAP THIRTEEN

©Crown Copyright 2005. All rights reserved. Licence Number 100011978

MAP FOURTEEN

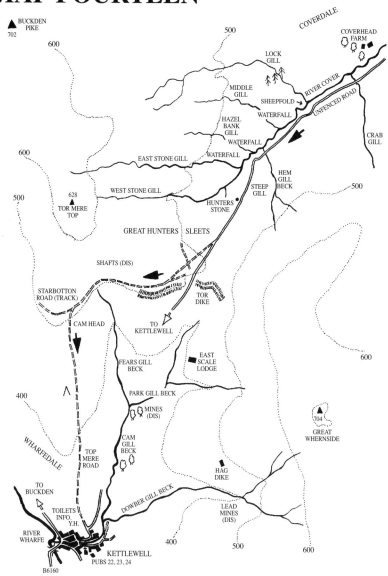

BUCKDEN
PIKE
702

600

500

COVERDALE

COVERHEAD
FARM

LOCK
GILL

MIDDLE
GILL

RIVER COVER

SHEEPFOLD

UNFENCED ROAD

WATERFALL

HAZEL
BANK
GILL

CRAB
GILL

WATERFALL

600

EAST STONE GILL

WATERFALL

HEM
GILL
BECK

500

WEST STONE GILL

STEEP
GILL

500

628

TOR MERE
TOP

HUNTERS
STONE

GREAT HUNTERS SLEETS

SHAFTS (DIS)

STARBOTTON
ROAD (TRACK)

TOR
DIKE

CAM HEAD

TO
KETTLEWELL

EAST
SCALE
LODGE

600

FEARS GILL
BECK

400

PARK GILL BECK

MINES
(DIS)

704

GREAT
WHERNSIDE

CAM
GILL
BECK

WHARFEDALE

TOP
MERE
ROAD

HAG
DIKE

TO
BUCKDEN

TOILETS
INFO.
Y.H.

DOWBER GILL BECK

LEAD
MINES
(DIS)

RIVER
WHARFE

400

500

600

KETTLEWELL
PUBS 22, 23, 24

B6160

©Crown Copyright 2005. All rights reserved. Licence Number 100011978

THE VALLEY OF WALDEN is a rarity for it does not have the suffix 'dale' in its name. This is a remote and hidden valley, the last retreat of the Celtic tribes fleeing from the invading Norse and Anglo-Saxons, indeed 'Walden' means 'Valley of the Welsh' as these native tribes were known. It is a valley of stark beauty, with steep gills cutting deep into the surrounding moorland reminiscent of neighbouring Coverdale. Walden Beck is born on the flanks of Buckden Pike, which dominates the dale head, and only has a short journey before it meets Bishopdale Beck just beyond West Burton. This steep-sided valley with its scattering of farmsteads has changed little over the centuries; you would be forgiven if you thought that you had stepped back in time. It is also one of the most remote and least visited valleys in the Dales, mainly due to the fact that only narrow 'dead end' farm lanes wind their way into its upper reaches. *"The valley does not display its beauty all at once: round each twist and bend it gives a fresh delight....There is no suggestion of a main way about the road up it, which was made not for outsiders to travel through, but for the people of the dale."* (**E. Pontefract & M. Hartley 'Wensleydale' 1936**). These roads serve the farms at Walden Head, with the curiously named Kentucky House, and Dovescar. Ancient packhorse routes lead out of the dale; from Walden Head a track heads over the southern shoulder of Buckden Pike to Starbotton in Wharfedale, and another track begins at Whiterow Farm and goes over Fleensop Moor to Horsehouse in Coverdale. Both are superb tracks rewarding the walker with breathtaking views. *"I am particularly in love with the narrow track on the east side of Walden and it is one of Helen's favourite places. To drive up there, high above the tree-lined Walden Beck, is to escape easily from the workaday world. And if you leave your car and walk the old path over the moor till the fell tilts into Coverdale and the vast stream-furrowed face of Little Whernside rears up across the valley, you will be richly rewarded."* (**J. Herriot 'James Herriot's Yorkshire' 1979**).

Set back from the road near to the entrance to Cote Farm are the remains of an old smelt mill chimney from the lead mining days – the surrounding moors are littered with the remains of lead and coal mines that date back to the 18th and 19th Centuries. Indeed, a glance at the map will reveal a plethora of old workings, shafts and even a colliery on Fleensop Moor, long since abandoned.

COVERDALE is a hauntingly beautiful valley of scattered farmsteads and attractive hamlets set amongst a wild landscape of high fells and deep ravines, known locally as gills, with the massive bulk of Great Whernside (704 metres) dominating the upper reaches of the valley. The word 'cover' is derived from the ancient British word that means 'a stream that flows through a deep ravine'. The river is born on the wild and lonely flanks of Tor Mere Top and Great Whernside, and flows for twelve miles to swell the waters of the River Ure just to the east of Middleham. *"Its seclusion has resulted in much intermarrying, and it is not to be wondered at that superstition has kept a hold here, that old customs and beliefs which have their origin in pagan days survive."* **(E. Pontefract & M. Hartley 1936).** The area between Horsehouse and the head of the valley, referred to locally as High Dale, makes up some of the most wild, bleak and desolate country in England. *"Around us is an amphitheatre of wild hills and mountains, whose dark crests stand forth boldly against white breezy clouds which are sweeping hurriedly across the sky, their shadows climbing hill after hill like skeletons of some gigantic army."* **(E. Bogg 'A Thousand Miles in Wharfedale' 1892).** It is hard to imagine that the road which winds its way precariously up the dale was once an important monastic route from Coverham Abbey over to Kettlewell where the monks owned some grazing land. This monastic road later became a busy packhorse route and was then used as part of the main stage coach route from London to Richmond; however the bone-shaking, not to mention nerve-jangling, journey over the very steep Park Rash Pass out of Kettlewell, with its hair-pin bend, was too much for some passengers and the route was soon changed. *"High up yonder, between Great Whernside and Buckden Pike, on the south and west, and Pen Hill on the north, the little River Cover has its birth, oozing out of the dark waste of moorland, which even to-day, is a vast solitude of unreclaimed land. Here during the thousand years of changeful destiny, from the incoming of the Roman to the Conquest of the Norman, this neck of land, was the scene of many fierce and sanguinary struggles. Other and more picturesque scenes,* *have no doubt, been often witnessed along this mountain road, cavalcades of knights, princes and prelates, and their numerous attendants; the Nevilles of Middleham and Raby; that celebrated figure of Warwick, the King-maker, and a host of others, who have left their names on the historic scroll, have passed and repassed over this wild mountain track to Middleham, Richmond, Raby, Brancepeth, etc."* (**E. Bogg 'Beautiful Wensleydale' 1925**).

The scattering of villages that lie along its length were originally settled by Viking farmers who made small clearings in the vast forest that once covered the entire dale; many of these Viking place-names survive including Caldbergh, Scrafton, Swineside, Arkleside and Gammersgill. This forest was later used by the Normans as a hunting forest and Carlton developed as its headquarters where Courts of the Forest were held. Carlton was also the home of Henry Constantine, a 19th Century local dialect poet. Caldbergh has literary connections as the birthplace of Miles Coverdale who first translated the Bible into English in 1535. The ruins of Coverham Abbey lie near the banks of the River Cover between Carlton and Middleham. Founded in 1212, the abbey once housed an abbot and sixteen canons who provided accommodation for travellers and employment for local people. Very little remains of the abbey mainly due to the stone being plundered to build local houses following the Dissolution of the Monasteries. *"The spirits of the monks seem still to hover around the ruined walls; they were lovers of beautiful nature, and chose their dwelling places with an artist's and a poet's eye. Though centuries have passed since they were driven forth, and their homes despoiled, yet their memory still lingers, and the charms of nature, art, and peaceful solitude which soothed their spirits still seem to cling around as we stand and muse within the ruined sanctuary."* (**E. Bogg 'From Eden Vale to the Plains of York'**). Guarding the entrance to Coverdale stands the majestic Middleham Castle, the 'Windsor of the North'. This castle dates back to Norman times and was the stronghold of the powerful Neville family, Earls of Warwick, for over 200 years from where they ruled their vast Northern estates virtually as a separate 'kingdom'. Richard Plantagenet, later the Duke of Gloucester then Richard III, grew up at the castle where he later met his wife Lady Anne Neville, the daughter of the Earl of Warwick (the Kingmaker). Their son Edward, Prince of Wales was born at the castle. Richard became king in 1483 but was killed at the Battle of Bosworth in 1485. The castle soon fell into disrepair and remained Crown property until 1625 when passed into private ownership. Much of the stonework was plundered in the 17th Century, thanks to Cromwell's destructive tendencies, and went to build local houses. The large 12th Century keep is second only to Tower of London in size. Today Middleham is a major centre for racehorse training with extensive gallops across Middleham Low Moor to the south west of the town, a tradition started by the monks of nearby Jervaulx Abbey. There are currently about 14 trainers in the Middleham area and over 200 horses.

The long descent from Fleensop Moor to Horsehouse in Coverdale reveals a wonderful panorama of the fells that encircle the 'High Dale' including Great Whernside, Little Whernside, Dead Man's Hill and Great Haw. Dead Man's Hill was the scene of a terrible murder in 1728, when a local innkeeper at Lodge just over the moors in Nidderdale killed three Scottish travelling tradesmen and buried their headless bodies on the moor above the inn, since when the particular stretch of moorland has been known as Dead Man's Hill. *"It was noticed too that the people at the inn seemed prosperous, and that many of the farmers in the district were using Scotch ponies and their wives wearing Paisley shawls. A search was made, and the bodies of the victims, all headless, were found buried near the house."* (**E. Pontefract & M. Hartley 1936**).

HORSEHOUSE *"... was famous in olden days, when packhorse trains left Knaresborough and there was open travel, not a wall to cross, a gate to open all the way to Scotland."* (**W. T. Palmer 'Odd Corners in the Yorkshire Dales' 1937**). Horsehouse, as the name implies, developed as an overnight stop for packhorses and stage coaches along the ancient route through the valley, and once boasted two inns to quench the thirst of the tired travellers. The Thwaite Arms, with its small rooms and stone flagged floors, still refreshes weary travellers;

however, the other inn, known as the King's Head, closed many years ago. *"A house high above the road was the other (inn); it has a long stone porch at the back of it where the men placed the food, and a hole in the garden, now partly filled in, was the dog pit where drovers' dogs were put for the night."* (**E. Pontefract & M. Hartley 1936**). The village developed further during the 19th Century with the development of small collieries on Fleensop Moor; several small miners' cottages can still be seen throughout the village. St Botolph's Church dates from the 15th Century when it was serviced by the monks of Coverham Abbey, however, the present building dates largely from a 'renovation' during the late 19th Century.

HIGH DALE is the name given to the wild upper reaches of Coverdale, *"The general characteristic of the dale is bleakness."* (**Fletcher 'Nooks and Corners of Yorkshire'**) There is, however, stark beauty in such wilderness *"...we look up the vale to Great Whernside, and through the autumn mists which lie along the vale we can see Little Whernside on the left, and on the right the heights of Buckden Pike, waves of sunlight tinge with golden the mighty billows of gloomy, purple moors."* (**E. Bogg**). The hamlets of High Dale, including Arkleside, Braidley, Woodale and Coverheads, are small farming communities that have changed little in centuries. The ground rises steadily for six miles from Horsehouse to the dale head where the road reaches a height of 503 metres; Great Whernside (704 m) and Buckden Pike (702 m) stand guard over the pass into Wharfedale. Near the highest point on the road stands Hunter's Stone, an inscribed medieval wayside guide-stone that was placed there by the monks of Coverham Abbey to help guide them over the moorland pass from Coverdale to their lands in Wharfedale. This stone reputedly possesses strange powers; when the clock strikes twelve at Hunter's Hall, otherwise known as Coverhead Farm which stands on the site of a hunting hall that belonged to the Lords of Middleham Castle, the stone spins round! The monastic route did not follow the now metalled road down to Kettlewell via Park Rash but branched off across the moors to drop down into Kettlewell by way of Top Mere Road; This walled track affords one of the finest views in the Yorkshire Dales with the sweeping valley of Wharfedale laid out before you and the rooftops of Kettlewell far below. *"It is said that the scenery and contour of the mountains around Kettlewell are nearly a fac-simile of the Valley of Jehosaphat, in Palestine."* (E. Bogg 1892).

GREAT WHERNSIDE towers above Upper Wharfedale, an immense mountainous shoulder of high moorland that separates Wharfedale from Nidderdale; this is Wharfedale's highest fell and one of the finest in the Yorkshire Dales. The boulder-strewn flat summit ridge is a rocky shelf of gritstone, punctuated by boulders and crags. This cap of gritstone across the high summit ridge sits on top of the underlying limestone strata that dominates the landscape of Upper Wharfedale – it is this gritstone that gave the mountain its name for Whernside means 'the hillside where millstones were got'. Great Whernside is often mistaken for Whernside above Ribblehead, which forms one of the famous Three Peaks of Yorkshire: Whernside (736 metres), Ingleborough (724 metres) and Pen-y-ghent (694 metres). Great Whernside is 10 metres higher than Pen-y-ghent with the added benefit of far fewer walkers aiming for its summit and some of the best fell-walking in the Yorkshire Dales.

TOR DIKE is a deep earthwork that stretches for almost a mile across the saddle of land known as Great Hunters Sleets between Great Whernside and Buckden Pike. This huge ditch and rampart once formed part of a defensive system built in around AD 70 by the early British Iron Age tribes, collectively known in the North of England as the Brigantes, in an attempt to prevent the Romans invading the northern Yorkshire Dales. Other Iron Age earthworks in the Dales include the ditches and ramparts near Grinton in Swaledale and the impressive hill-fort on the summit of Ingleborough. *"Legend says, this place was formerly the habitation of spirits supposed to have been ghosts of slain warriors hovering around the battleground."* (**E. Bogg 1892**). Unfortunately these defences were not enough to stop the Romans. We now sadly leave Coverdale to return to Wharfedale, *"As we leave Leyburn we get a most beautiful view up Coverdale, with the two Whernsides standing out most conspicuously at the head of the valley, and it is this last view of Coverdale, and the great valley from which it branches, that remains in the mind as one of the finest pictures of this most remarkable portion of Yorkshire."* (**G. Home 'Yorkshire' 1908**).

KETTLEWELL is one of the finest villages in the Yorkshire Dales, a delightful cluster of old cottages and inns sheltered in the side-valley of Cam Gill Beck near its confluence with the River Wharfe. A maze of lanes and paths entice you to explore the heart of the village which straddles Cam Gill Beck some distance up into the deep cleft of its valley, with numerous old bridges spanning the fast-flowing waters. First settled by a Norse-Irish chieftain called 'Ketel' back in the 9th Century, the village grew in importance following the granting of lands in the area as well as part of the Manor of Kettlewell to the monks of Coverham Abbey in the 12th Century; the other half of the manor was granted to the Nevilles of Middleham. Fountains Abbey and Bolton Priory also owned land nearby which, combined with its strategic location at the junction of several important routes, meant that Kettlewell quickly grew into an important trading centre and was granted a market charter in the 13th Century. These routes included the old Roman road from Ilkley to Bainbridge, the monastic route over to Coverham Abbey via Top Mere Road, numerous packhorse trails and, later, the stagecoach route from London, all of which brought a steady stream of travellers, drovers and tradesmen into the village – it also lay on the edge of the Norman hunting forest of Langstrothdale Chase. Following the Dissolution of the Monasteries in the 16th Century, Coverham Abbey forfeited the Manor of Kettlewell and associated lands around Kettlewell to the Crown. A few decades later the lands held by the Neville family were also forfeited following the ill-fated Rising of the North in 1569, when sympathetic Catholic lords and noblemen of Northern England rose up against Elizabeth I. In 1656 the manor was sold to a group of local men who became the Trust Lords of Kettlewell. These Trust Lords were elected from the freeholders to ensure that the manorial dues and rights were kept in trust. *"The result of this was that there grew up here a community of important yeomen, taking part in the life of the district, and giving a certain amount of affluence to it."* (**E. Pontefract & M. Hartley 'Wharfedale' 1938**). The Trust Lords still draw income from land that they own and use the money for improvements in the village.

Lead mining and textiles in the 18th and 19th Centuries brought new prosperity to Kettlewell; most of the houses in the village date from this period, although a handful of 17th Century houses remain. Behind the village can be seen the remains of a smelting mill which was used from 1700 to 1886. It was during this time that Kettlewell grew into a bustling village with as many as thirteen inns to accommodate the market-goers, miners and travellers. The market lapsed long ago, however, three inns remain including the King's Head with its wonderful inglenook fireplace, the Blue Bell Inn which dates back to 1680 and was originally a coaching inn that takes its name from one of the old stagecoach companies. Across the road from the Blue Bell Inn stands the Racehorses Hotel, which was once used as the stables for the stagecoaches as the 'trace horses' were used to pull the coaches up the steep Park Rash Pass behind the village. *"Its comfortable little inns make Kettlewell a very fine centre for rambles in the wild dales that run up towards the head of Wharfedale."* (**G. Home 1908**). The Church of St Mary dates back to Norman times, however, it was demolished in 1882 and a new Victorian church built. Only the Norman font is original complete with a carving of a boar's head, the badge of the Neville family. The church does have many notable features including a framed document dating from 1380 concerning the monks of Coverham Abbey as well as unusual stained glass depicting the Battle of the Somme - look out for the gravestone of a man who died in 1770 at the ripe old age of 117!

Today, Kettlewell is a thriving village that retains its own identity despite the large number of visitors. Not only is it one of the finest bases in the Yorkshire Dales for walking with superb paths radiating in every direction, but it also hosts a popular scarecrow festival every August and was recently used as a location in the hit film 'Calendar Girls'. *"But one can easily mark the change coming over the scene; the screech of the railway engine is gradually drawing nearer, and many are the aliens seeking to obtain a foothold in this isolated dale within a dale. The electric light is already an installed fact - here as well as Grassington."* (**E. Bogg 'By the Banks of the Wharfe' 1921**). It is worth spending time exploring the alleys and lanes that make up Kettlewell to discover its three inns, shops, youth hostel, Post Office, cafes, church, maypole and the beck which runs through it plus lots more.

KETTLEWELL
to
GRASSINGTON

✦

"The Yorkshire highlands, raking up to wide-flung mountain fastnesses, lie remote from usual haunts; and their people are rooted in free, unspoiled acres. There is only the one road to knowledge of the Dales and Dalesfolk - lifelong intimacy with the rugged scarps, the hidden glens, the homesteads, big and little, perched on the mountains' feet or gathered into grey, comely villages. Here and there a market town is busy with agriculture's pleasant merchandise. Never are men far from the overwatching moors, whose minstrels are the plover and curlew, grouse and hoarse hoodie-crow. Land and people have grown into a sure, ripe communion, and to be admitted to their fellowship is to learn the deeper things that reach the true romance. Legend and history mingle with the everyday of human intercourse. Storm and shine, the nor'-easter's bite on sleety uplands, the fragrance of swathed hayfields when summer dusks steal down about a land of plenty, the gypsies' caravans, slow-winding through a country friendly to them from the ancient days - who shall tell what goes to the Dales' full glamour?"

H. Sutcliffe
'The Striding Dales' 1929.

WALK INFORMATION

Points of interest: Ancient 'green lanes', far-reaching views, deserted long-houses, numerous abandoned lead mines, the swaying bridge across the Wharfe, the hidden village of the cobblers, '101 ways to cross a stream' and the powerful force of Linton Falls.

Distance:

Kettlewell to Hebden	9 miles
Hebden to Grassington	3 miles
Total	12 miles

Time: Allow 6 hours

Terrain: The section from Kettlewell to Yarnbury follows high-level grassy moorland paths and tracks across Conistone Moor rising up to Capplestone Gate (512 metres), with rough and boggy terrain in places as well as a number of ascents and descents. From Yarnbury, clear miners' tracks lead through an area of old lead mines then down through Hebden Gill alongside Hebden Beck. The section from Hebden to Grassington follows quiet country lanes and clear paths across meadowland, with a suspension bridge across the River Wharfe to the south of Hebden and a footbridge across the Wharfe above Linton Falls back into Grassington.

The initial climb out of Kettlewell is quite steep. The moorland around Capplestone Gate is exposed to the elements as well as rough and rocky underfoot in places. Do not explore the old mine workings at Yarnbury. There are stepping stones across Hebden Beck, which may be difficult after heavy rain. Take care walking along the country lanes around Hebden, Thorpe and Linton.

Ascents:	Capplestone Gate:	512 metres

Viewpoints:	Ascent from Kettlewell up onto Conistone Moor affords wonderful views of Upper Wharfedale. Extensive views from Capplestone Gate. The track from Bare House to Yarnbury affords good views down Wharfedale. Lead mining remains throughout Hebden Gill. Final descent from Thorpe Lane towards Linton affords good views across the valley towards Grassington.

FACILITIES

Kettlewell	Inn / B&B / Shop / P.O. / Café / Bus / Phone / Toilets / YH / Camp
Hebden	Inn / B&B / Shop / P.O. / Café / Bus / Phone
Thorpe	B&B
Linton	Inn / B&B / Bus / Phone
Linton Falls	Toilets
Grassington	Inn / B&B / Shop / P.O. / Café / Bus / Phone / Toilets / Info

ROUTE DESCRIPTION

(Map fifteen)

Leave Kettlewell along the lane to the right of the bridge (and stream) across Cam Gill Beck near to the Kings Head pub. Follow this lane up with Cam Gill Beck on your left then, just after you have left the houses behind, take the stony track slanting steeply up to the right (SP 'Whernside Pastures') to quickly reach a gate. Head through the gate and follow the stony track climbing steeply up (alongside the wall on your left) then bearing steeply up to the right and levelling out slightly (with Dowber Gill Beck falling steeply away to your left) heading gradually up to reach a second gate (SP). After the gate, continue straight on up along the track then, where the track forks after 150 yards, follow the left-hand track winding steeply up to reach a third gate in a stone wall up to your left (SP). Head through this gate then turn immediately right along an indistinct grassy track alongside the wall on your right *(several tracks to choose from – do not follow the clear rutted track)*. Carry straight on gently rising up alongside this wall on your right (keep close to the wall on your right – ignore any tracks off to the left) then, after 0.25 miles, follow the wide grassy path bearing very slightly away from the wall heading straight on across the middle of the field (wall now just across to your right) gently rising up for a further 0.25 miles to reach a ladder stile across a wall ahead. Cross this ladder stile then continue straight on along a grassy path bearing slightly to the left across the field to reach a stone wall-stile, after which head across the next field to reach a second stone wall-stile. After this stile, head straight on along the grassy path for 150 yards to join a wide grassy path which you follow straight on rising up onto the top of a low grassy/limestone ridge then follow the grassy path across the flat shelf of land to soon reach a fork in the path, where you bear to the right to reach a ladder-stile over a stone wall (SP). After the ladder-stile, continue straight on along the grassy path bearing to the left across the gently sloping hillside up to reach a ladder stile in the top left corner of the field (SP), after which carry straight on along the narrow path bearing slightly to the left up onto a low ridge above some limestone outcrops *(ignore the gate in the wall up to your left on the top of the ridge)* then follow the grassy path along the top of this low ridge above the limestone outcrops (passing a right-angle in the wall down to your right) then continue straight on across the rough grassy moorland bearing very slightly to the left to reach a ladder stile over a wall across your path (with a ridge of gritstone boulders and crags up to your left). After this ladder-stile, follow the path bearing slightly to the left up across the rough field to reach a stile beside a gate towards the top left corner of the field that brings you out into an area of mining debris and spoil heaps. Bear up to the left across the spoil heaps to quickly reach a 3-finger signpost where you take the footpath to the right (SP 'Conistone') which heads across spoil heaps and rough ground (yellow waymarker posts) to soon reach the top of a low gritstone ridge (small boulders and low outcrops) just above a stone wall down to your right. Follow this gritstone ridge heading straight on (slightly to the left) with the wall on your right for 0.25 miles to reach a ladder stile beside a gate in this wall on your right at Capplestone Gate - SE 002 699 *(Trig Point just across the wall hidden from view).*

Cross the ladder stile and follow the clear grassy track winding gently down across the hillside (Conistone Turf Road) then bending more steeply down to the left through a large gap in a stone wall (limestone crags to your left and two small conifer plantations down to your right), after which follow the clear track slanting down across the hillside to join a wall on your left (on the other side of the field) which you follow down passing to the left-side of the (lower) plantation to reach a gate across the grassy track at the bottom end of the plantation. Head through the gate and walk straight on for a short distance then turn left (SP) and follow the grassy track straight on across the middle of the field to reach a gate in the far right corner that leads onto a walled stony track (Bycliffe Road). Turn right along the track (SP 'Conistone') and follow this down through a gate at the end of the walled track, after which continue along the track down passing through a wide cleft in the limestone pavements just after which turn left off the track down through a gate in a wall (SP 'Dales Way Grassington'). Head through the gate and follow the clear grassy/stony track straight on skirting above the top of the dry limestone valley of Conistone Dib then across the rough pasture to reach a wall stile, after which take the FP that branches up to the left (not signposted) to reach a gate in a wall – *do not continue along the wide grassy path of the Dales Way.* After the wall gate, cross the wall-stile to the right then head diagonally left up across the hillside to reach a gate in the far left-hand corner of the field (near to a small wood). After the gate, continue along the path keeping close to the wall on your right, through a wall gap (passing the small wood on your right) and continue alongside the wall on your right passing below some limestone outcrops, after which follow the path steeply up the hillside to the left to reach the deserted Bare House Farm (SE 005 669).

Head straight on keeping the farm and its walled enclosures to your right – the path soon becomes a grassy track which you follow curving round to the right (alongside the stone wall) to reach a gate beside an old stone barn. Head through the gate and follow the track straight on to reach another gate that leads onto a clear track. Follow this stony track straight on (to the right), through another gate then follow the walled track down for 1 mile to reach a clear stony track (Moor Lane) across your path near the houses at Yarnbury. Turn right along the track for a short distance then turn left opposite Yarnbury House over a cattle grid (SP 'Hebden') along a track heading through the old lead mining area. Follow this track straight on winding through the old workings (information boards) for 0.3 miles then, where the track forks (Cupola Chimney in the distance), follow the right-hand track down through a large gap in a stone wall then straight on (ignore the two tracks off to the right) passing more spoil heaps to reach a gate in a stone wall. After the gate, follow the stony track to the left winding steeply down into Hebden Gill then, as you reach the valley bottom, follow the track to the right heading down alongside Hebden Beck on your left, over a spoil heap then across two fords to reach a gate across your path beside Hebden Beck (wooden guard across the stream) - SE 026 653. Head through the gate and continue along the streamside path for 100 yards then cross the stepping stones over the stream after which head down with the stream now on your right across more spoil heaps to quickly reach a gate just before some ruinous mine buildings (Hebden Mines dressing floor). Head through the gate and follow the clear track heading down through Hebden Gill with the stream on your right for 0.75 miles, over a stone bridge across the stream and into the hamlet of Hole Bottom. Head straight on along the road and follow this down into Hebden.

At the cross-roads with the B6265 in the centre of Hebden, head straight on (SP 'Burnsall') passing the shop on your right and follow this road out of the village. Continue along the road bending down to the left then take the FP to the right (SP 'Burnsall, Thorpe Lane,

B6160') and cross the suspension bridge across the River Wharfe (SE 025 623). After the bridge, turn left then almost immediately right through a bridlegate in a fence (SP 'Thorpe Lane') and follow the path slanting up across the hillside to reach another bridlegate at the top of the wooded bank. Head through the bridlegate, and follow the grassy path straight on bearing slightly to the right to reach a gate in a wall, after which head straight on alongside the wall on your left to reach the main road. Cross this road and follow the lane opposite into Thorpe. Follow the road bearing to the right through the village (passing the small triangular green on your left) and rising up to the right out of the village then, as you reach the edge of the village, take the turning to the left. Follow this narrow walled lane for about 0.5 miles *(ignore the first FP to the right 'BW to B6160')* then take the FP to the right over a wall stile just before the ruined stone barn (SP 'Linton') - SE 005 621. Head straight on across the field, keeping fairly close to the wall on your left, passing a small wood on your left then head straight on down across the hillside to reach a ladder stile beside a gate. Cross the stile and head straight on down along the track then, as you approach the farm buildings on the outskirts of Linton, turn right through a bridle-gate beside a field gate (SP 'Linton') then left alongside the wall and follow the clearly marked path through two more bridle-gates then along a track skirting behind the farmhouse (Grange Farm) to quickly join a metalled lane at the entrance to the farm. Follow this lane to the right into Linton. Walk through the village with the stream on your left then, at the T-junction with the main road (beside the road-bridge), turn right and follow this road up out of Linton straight on to reach a crossroads with the B6160. Head straight on at the crossroads down towards Linton Parish Church then, where the road bends to the left over Bow Bridge, take the turning to the right straight on (Church Road) then, after a short distance where the road bends to the right, take the path to the left just before the houses (SP 'Grassington via Linton Falls'). Follow the clear path skirting around the houses (do not cross the old stone packhorse bridge) then over the large FB across Linton Falls (SE 001 633) and straight on along the enclosed path back up into Grassington.

MAP FIFTEEN

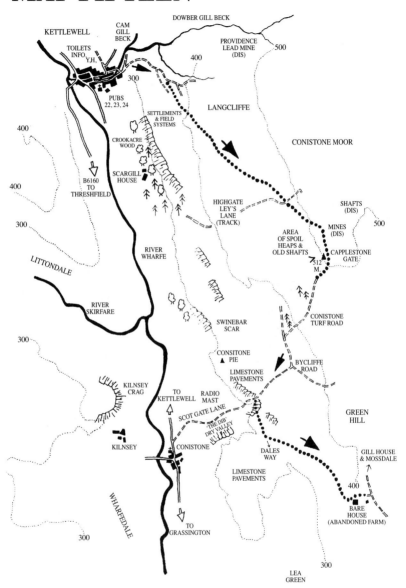

KETTLEWELL

CAM GILL BECK

DOWBER GILL BECK

TOILETS
INFO Y.H.

PROVIDENCE
LEAD MINE
(DIS)

400

500

300

PUBS
22, 23, 24

LANGCLIFFE

SETTLEMENTS
& FIELD
SYSTEMS

CONISTONE MOOR

CROOKACRE
WOOD

400

B6160
TO
THRESHFIELD

400

SCARGILL
HOUSE

HIGHGATE
LEY'S
LANE
(TRACK)

SHAFTS
(DIS)

MINES
(DIS)

500

300

RIVER
WHARFE

AREA
OF SPOIL
HEAPS &
OLD SHAFTS

512
M.

CAPPLESTONE
GATE

LITTONDALE

RIVER
SKIRFARE

SWINEBAR
SCAR

CONISTONE
TURF ROAD

300

CONISTONE
▲ PIE

LIMESTONE
PAVEMENTS

BYCLIFFE
ROAD

KILNSEY
CRAG

TO
KETTLEWELL

RADIO
MAST

GREEN
HILL

SCOT GATE LANE

THE DIB
DRY VALLEY

KILNSEY

CONISTONE

DALES
WAY

GILL HOUSE
& MOSSDALE

LIMESTONE
PAVEMENTS

400

WHARFEDALE

BARE
HOUSE
(ABANDONED FARM)

300

TO
GRASSINGTON

300

LEA
GREEN

©Crown Copyright 2005. All rights reserved. Licence Number 100011978

MAP SIXTEEN

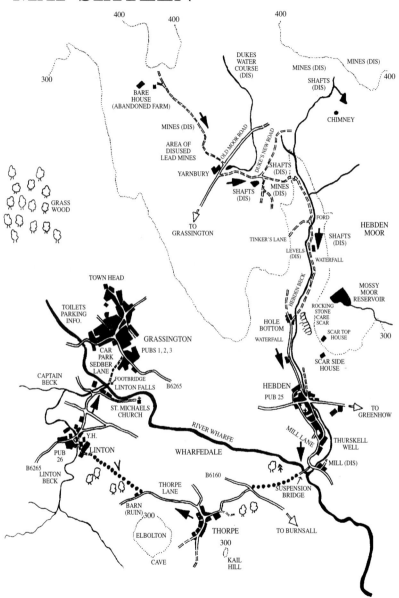

©Crown Copyright 2005. All rights reserved. Licence Number 100011978

CONISTONE MOOR is criss-crossed by old packhorse routes as well as more modern long distance walks. This is because the village of Conistone has marked an important crossing point of the Wharfe for centuries; Conistone Bridge was originally constructed in monastic times as part of the route from Fountains Abbey to the grazing lands in the Lake District via Mastiles Lane. Bycliffe Road is a superb green lane which climbs over Conistone Moor to reach Middlesmoor in Nidderdale. The Conistone Turf Road links Conistone with the lower slopes of Great Whernside where peat was once cut, dried and then used as fuel in the houses of Upper Wharfedale. *"These paths are nearly as old as the hills and have been trod for centuries, and are the heritage of every free-born Briton."* (**E. Bogg 'By the Banks of the Wharfe' 1921**). The 84 mile 'Dales Way' also crosses Conistone Moor on its way from Ilkley to Bowness-on-Windermere. The panorama from Capplestone Gate is extensive with views over Wharfedale and beyond to Pendle Hill, Pen-y-Ghent, Fountains Fell, Yockenthwaite Moor and Buckden Pike. To the east Conistone Moor stretches away as far as the eye can see, a vast landscape of rolling heather moorland that separates Nidderdale from Wharfedale with the indistinct 'rise' of Meugher (575 m), pronounced 'moo-fer', which is said to be the most remote fell-top in the Yorkshire Dales, whilst to the north the great bulk of the Great Whernside summit ridge gradually rises up.

BARE HOUSE, also known as Barras, is a deserted farmhouse situated high on the hills near to Yarnbury. The name is derived from the Norse 'bargh-hus' meaning 'hill farm' as the early Norse settlers chose isolated moorland locations for their farms. The monks from Fountains Abbey had a farm here, although following the Dissolution of the Monasteries the tenant farmer would have been able to purchase the property. These farmers became relatively affluent and subsequently the farm was rebuilt in 1620. Bare House is a good example of a long house with living accommodation and barn all under the same roof. The walled lane from Yarnbury to Bare House (known as Lime Kiln Lane) affords good views of these windswept uplands. *"Follow this rough cart-road until you reach a gate which leads to* *the moor. Pass through, and pause a few moments to view the landscape, which at this point is superb – a very Kaleidoscope of contrasts under the changing conditions of sun and cloud overhead. On the right you have a view of the treeless valley of Mossdale, with Whernside in the background. On the left you see, a field or two away, Barras."* (**J. Crowther 'Rambles Round Grassington' 1920).** Lime Kiln Lane continues past Bare House across the moors to eventually reach Gill House, one of the most solitary farmhouses in the Dales, now sadly uninhabited and dilapidated. *"In a clump of trees to the right is the lonely farm of Gill House, where the inhabitants often wake up on a winters morning to find the snow up to their bedroom windows."* (**E. Pontefract & M. Hartley 'Wharfedale' 1938).** Beyond Gill House there is nothing but bleak, wild, unenclosed moorland for several miles before dropping down into Nidderdale.

YARNBURY was the home of the mining manager and the administrative centre for the extensive lead mining activities that once took place across the surrounding moorland; the former Mine Agent's house, workshops, weigh house, powder house and old smithy can still be seen. This area is littered with the remains of the lead mining industry which flourished during the 18th and 19th Centuries. Lead has been mined in Wharfedale since Roman times at nearby Greenhow, although it was the monks of Fountains Abbey who first mined lead on Grassington Moor back in the 15th Century when they also operated a small smelt mill here. It was not until 1604 that mining began in earnest when Lord Clifford of Skipton Castle, the 4th Earl of Cumberland, built a smelt mill along the banks of the River Wharfe near Linton and began to work the mines. The Earl granted individual miners small plots of land some 30-yards in length, known as meers, where they dug down along the line of a mineral vein, sharing the profits from any smelted lead with the Earl. Dozens of these early shallow shafts, known as bell pits, can still be seen scattered across Grassington Moor. This system of mining continued for several decades but by the 1760s many of the shafts had reached the water table and production slumped. In the mid 18th Century the Duke of Devonshire inherited the manor of Grassington and associated mineral rights through marriage and so encouraged deeper shafts and new exploration of mineral veins by extending the mining area, granting the miners leases and building the new Cupola smelt mill in 1792. This only had a limited impact and so the decision was made in 1796 to excavate an adit, or drainage tunnel, to drain water from the Yarnbury mining field into Hebden Beck, thus lowering the water table. This was back-breaking work that took over thirty years to complete.

However, the high water table remained an obstacle throughout the early 19th Century and it was not until John Taylor was made the Duke's mine agent in 1818 that lead mining really began to flourish. He built a series of dams across the moors that brought water to the mining field via the six-mile long Duke's Water Course, which provided water-power to drive around a dozen waterwheels that in turn powered pumps to drain the shafts and levels, thus allowing mining to resume a decade before the drainage adit was completed. He also sank new deeper shafts and built roads between the mines, dressing floors (where the ore was crushed and separated) and smelt mill. Over the next few decades, Taylor also extended the network of reservoirs and watercourses to provided power to drive the pumps, and also built the Cupola Smelt Mill Chimney and associated long flue in 1849 to improve to the efficiency of the smelt mill and help disperse the poisonous fumes; the chimney stands 60 feet high and is an unmistakable landmark for miles around. The mines were at their most productive between 1821 and 1861 when around 170 miners produced almost 1,000 tons of lead annually. *"Occasionally a faint knocking sound is heard in old mines. The miners believed that this was made by the ghosts of men killed in the mines, and that it came as a warning of an accident. They would leave off work for the day if they heard the knockers'."* **(E. Pontefract & M. Hartley 1938).** Unfortunately, most of the new shafts that were sunk during this period in search of new rich veins proved unsuccessful and so, after 1861, output steadily fell as the reserves became exhausted. Lead mining finally came to an end on Grassington Moor in 1880 as cheaper imports and dwindling reserves meant that the mines were no longer viable. *"The lead mines,* *from what one sees during this walk, covered a large area. They had good buildings, and must have employed a large number of workpeople. Special attention appears to have been given to the making of levels to drain the water from the mines on the moors during mining operations some 60 years ago."* **(J. Crowther 1920).** The numerous shafts, spoil heaps and ruinous buildings stand as a silent tribute to the men who once worked in these inhospitable uplands. Information boards and a marked Lead Mining Trail help explain the crumbling ruins. Extreme care must be taken when exploring this area.

HEBDEN GILL leads down from Grassington Moor to the village of Hebden. The Gill is steep-sided and narrow with the fast-flowing Hebden Beck competing with the old miners' track for space along the valley floor. Again, there are numerous crumbling relics of the lead mining industry all around including several levels and the remains of the Hebden Mines dressing floor where lead ore was crushed prior to being sent to the smelt mill further down the valley near Hole Bottom. *"Away upwards, we climb under the shadow of immense rock; the large mass which peers over the valley is named the Rocking Stone, and can be moved, the natives say, by a slight pressure. Upwards still, the mines are reached; curious old holes and shafts are to be seen near the torrent, which at this place flows over a shelf of rock. Still upwards, all signs of humanity are left behind, and we tread the wild, wild moorland; even the stone walls which spoil many a rugged landscape are left."* **(E. Bogg 'A Thousand Miles in Wharfedale' 1892).** Beyond Hole Bottom, just out of sight from the road, is a waterfall known as Scala Force which has a beautiful setting in a wooded gorge.

HEBDEN is situated in the sheltered valley of Hebden Gill beside the ancient crossing point over Hebden Beck. The settlement was first established in Saxon times for its name means 'valley where rose-hips grow' in Old English. *"Its glory is its setting by a deep wooded glen, where the Hebden Beck comes from a pretty waterfall on its way to the Wharfe. There are two bridges side by side, the big one carrying the moorland road. The old houses and the century-old church look up to the enfolding hills, and from the rocky crags across the stream is a wonderful*

panorama of mountain scenery." (**A. Mee 'Yorkshire West Riding'
1941**). The road which runs east to west through the heart of the
village is an ancient route, possibly prehistoric, which was used during
medieval times by the monks of Fountains Abbey to get to their
grazing lands above Kilnsey. This important route later became busy
with drovers and packhorses when it was known as the High Road
that linked the important market towns and villages of Craven with
Ripon and York. The old bridge across Hebden Beck was washed
away by floods and rebuilt in the 17th and then again in the 18th
Century then, in the late 18th Century, the Pateley Bridge to
Grassington Turnpike road was opened with a new bridge built across
Hebden Beck, which in turn was replaced by the present road bridge
just downstream in 1827. There appears to have been two quite
distinct settlements at Hebden. The first was centred on the river
crossing, a cluster of cottages and farms set haphazardly around the
old bridge across Hebden Beck. The second was a planned medieval
settlement laid out by the lord of the manor. This consisted of a row
of small farmsteads that faced onto the main street with small strips
of land known as tofts running back from them, which were enclosed
by a back lane. Beyond this back lane were the communal village
fields. This medieval layout remains intact and can be clearly seen on
the map, although the old houses were replaced with rows of miners'
cottages and many of the tofts in-filled during the lead mining boom
of the 19th Century. As the old feudal system disappeared and
prosperity increased during the 17th Century, many of these new
yeoman farmers rebuilt their houses in stone, several of which can still
be seen.

The real growth period began in the early 19th Century as more
people came to the area to seek work in the local lead mines. Most of
the village dates from this period including the replacement bridge,
the church of 1841 and the school in 1875 as well as numerous
miners' cottages, *"Lead mining, which formerly gave employment to many
of the people, having now become unprofitable, has been the cause of the
decrease of the inhabitants – hence the reason of the many tenantless houses
in the village."* (**E. Bogg 1892**). There has been a corn mill at Hebden

since medieval times, situated along the banks of Hebden Beck near its confluence with the River Wharfe just to the south of the village. This was superseded by a cotton mill in the late 18th Century, which continued production until 1870. Subsequent owners tried to revive the mill's fortunes, and it later produced hydroelectric for the village, before finally closing. It was demolished in 1967, although a row of millworkers' cottages remain. Thurskell Well is a rare example of a well which still retains its pagan god dedication to Thor, a name that dates back to Norse times; most wells have been Christianised over the centuries, *"Here people assembled to worship and partake of the water, as communicants, to-day, do of wine."* (**E. Bogg 1921**). *"One can imagine that the strangeness of life-giving water coming apparently from nowhere through a rock or mossy patch in the hillside would, to primitive people with their eye for essential truth, seem like a miracle - an appearance of something divine. So the custom of 'well-dressings', and the joyous festival in connection with them, go back to prehistoric times. Thruskell is famed for its gushing water and also for having kept its original name, the fountain of Thor."* (**C. E. Lewis 'Wharfedale'**). I recommend the excellent Timothy Taylor's beers at the Clarendon Hotel to quench your thirst rather than the well water.

The stepping stones across the River Wharfe were built to allow villagers from Thorpe access to the corn mill on the north bank of the river. The adjacent suspension bridge was built in 1885 by the village blacksmith to allow a safer crossing of the river following a drowning accident.

THORPE lies hidden between the grassy hills of Elbolton and Kail and is not visible from any part of Wharfedale; your first view of the village is when you are actually entering it. It is a quiet, sleepy village with a handful of old farms, barns and houses clustered around a small triangular green. *"The first view of the place is astonishing; approach by whatever side you will it is so completely hidden by surrounding fells, over whose solitary wastes the eye is ranging, when, like a dream or oasis in the desert, this old time village spreads before us."* (**E. Bogg 1892**). The bright green hills which help conceal Thorpe are actually limestone reef knolls, formed 300 million years ago when this area was submerged beneath a warm, tropical sea. Coral reefs developed within this sea, which over millions of years built up to form an area of more resistant limestone that has created these conical hills. The eastern slopes of these hills boasts some of the finest examples of preserved medieval ploughing terraces, known as lynchets, in the Yorkshire Dales. *"On the summit of the hill called Elbolton, high above the little village of Thorpe, evidence has been found of sunworship being practised there. Even to this day there is, amongst the older folk of the district, a certain amount of belief in fairies and ghosts, and places are pointed out on the hillsides where they are said to dance."* (Fletcher 'Nooks and Corners of Yorkshire'). For such a small place Thorpe has a fascinating history. The village was a safe haven for people of the dale against Scottish raiders during the 14th and 15th Centuries. Thorpe was also reputedly the home of very highly skilled shoemakers who first started making shoes for the monks of Fountains Abbey. *"After the Abbeys were dissolved the shoemakers went on working in Thorpe - at one time there were forty of them - and it became famous for its fine shoes. People would travel long distances to get a pair fitted and made here. An old woman who died only a few years ago used to tell how she rode over from Grassington as a young woman to be measured for shoes at Thorpe. Her father was a Grassington shoemaker himself, but she said there were no shoes like Thorpe shoes. As late as 1822 there were two shoemakers and one bootmaker at Thorpe. The last of the old craftsmen, Kit Inman, died two years ago at Burnsall, and there is not even a cobbler now."* (M. Hartley & E. Pontefract 1938).

Elbolton Cave, also known as Knave Knoll Hole but locally known as Navvy Noddle Hole, is a cave situated on the south-eastern side of Elbolton Hill in which human remains and fragments of Neolithic pottery were discovered in the late 19th Century that date back between 2,000 and 3,000 years alongside Arctic animals including wolves, bears and reindeer; a reminder of the Dales landscape after the last Ice Age. *"Above the village is Elbolton Hill 1,100 feet high, with a cave where extinct animals once sheltered, and where the bones of 12 men sitting in a ring were found 20 centuries after they had died."* (A. Mee 1941).

LINTON, often known by its Sunday name of Linton-in-Craven, is a fine example of an Anglian settlement with stone houses facing onto a large green. Linton Beck, which flows through the village, is crossed by a multitude of bridges, including a road bridge, clapper bridge, packhorse bridge, stepping stones and fords, *"Perhaps there is some magical significance in crossing the water."* (**N. Duerden** **'Portrait of the Dales' 1978).** It is easy to understand why the village was voted 'Loveliest in the North' by the News Chronicle in 1949 as the stream, packhorse bridge, green and old houses. including a classic Dales' inn, create an attractive scene. *"Linton ...is a charmingly characteristic Craven village, its dwellings clustered pleasantly around the green. A stream barely deep enough to cover its pebbles, ripples and wimples through the centre of the spacious 'green'; yet this same stream at flood is so forceful as to formerly make crossing it dangerous to man or beast."* (**E. Bogg 1921).**

Dominating the village is the Fountaine Hospital which was founded and endowed in 1721 with money from the will of Richard Fountaine to provide almshouses for six poor people of the parish as well as a small chapel. Richard Fountaine was a local man who made his fortune as a timber merchant and coffin maker in London during the Plague of 1665 and the Great Fire of 1666 and became an Alderman of the City of London. The Fountaine Trust continues to draw income for the almshouses from land it owns in the area, and the Hospital still provides accommodation for local elderly people. The building was reputedly designed by Sir John Vanbrugh, who also designed Castle Howard, and introduced the Classical style of building to the Dales. *"There is a maypole on the green, and at one end are the imposing almshouses founded in the 18th century and enlarged in the 19th, looking like a little town hall with their domed tower."* (**A. Mee 1941).** Other notable buildings in the village are the Old Hall, which dates from the 17th Century with Georgian extensions, and White Abbey, a fine example of a 17th Century yeoman's house that was once the home of the famous Dales author Halliwell Sutcliffe. A small glacial lake once filled the flat fields behind the village, these marshy conditions were ideal for the growing of flax from which linen was made, indeed the name Linton is probably derived from the Anglo-Saxon 'lin' meaning flax and 'tun' meaning enclosure. Flax was last grown in the early 19th Century and sadly the lake was drained around 1850. *"The tarn has gone now, and no flax waves here, and the valley seems to wait and listen pathetically, as if it wished the old busy times back again."* (E. Pontefract & M. Hartley 1938).

LINTON CHURCH, dedicated to St Michael and All Angels, has a lovely setting beside River Wharfe half a mile from the village, and serves the villages of Linton, Grassington, Hebden and Threshfield as it has done for centuries; a path leads from each village to the church. It is an ancient building that dates back to the 12th Century with many original Norman features, although much modification took place in the 14th and 15th Centuries – look out for the medieval roof boss that depicts the pagan symbol of the green man. It is built in characteristic Dales style; long and low with a bell turret rather than a tower to call the faithful. But why was this church built in such a remote riverside setting so far from the villages it serves? The most probable answer is that it was built upon the site of an ancient pagan religious shrine.

LINTON FALLS make an impressive end to this walk, as the River Wharfe tumbles spectacularly over rocks caused by the Craven Fault, an impressive sight after heavy rain, *"At flood time the Wharfe at Linton 'falls', in its wild impetuous rush, is hurled over the obstructive rocks that make the 'rapids' with thunderous roar, the grey clouds of spray and foam flung forth adds a feeling of awe to the weird effect."* (E. Bogg 1921). Note the weir and old mill race which once provided power for Linton Mill before it closed in 1959. A mill has stood on this site since medieval times, however, the old mill buildings were demolished and new houses built in the 1980s, although some millworkers' cottages remain.

Take time to pause on the bridge above Linton Falls, and reflect upon what you have just achieved. Grassington, the final destination of this walk, lies just a few minutes away, but a walk is all about the journey, not the destination. What may have started as plain facts and figures – seventy-six miles over six days – has grown with every step into a whole experience. You will now walk back into Grassington richer for your experience, with a little piece of the Yorkshire Dales embedded in your soul and memories that will last a lifetime. Memories of the high fells and heather moors, spectacular waterfalls, cosy pubs, crumbling lead mines and distant horizons. *"I walked along the busy streets to the station, aware of my curious glances, for my clothes were unkempt and dirty, and my shoes, with heels gone and soles barely holding on, were so fast falling to pieces that I had to slide my feet as I walked lest they fall completely asunder. I was a spectre from a midden, but I marched in triumph...Respectability is often regarded as a matter of starch; hill-wandering takes all the starch out of a man, first out of his clothes, then out of his soul. And note, this cleansing process does not leave him limp, but gives him strength and a new vision."* **(A Wainwright 'A Pennine Journey - The Story of a Long Walk in 1938' 1986).**

BIBLIOGRAPHY

The following books are listed as follows: author, title, date first published and publisher.

T. Shaw, 'The History of Wharfedale', 1830, William Walker.

E. Bogg, 'A Thousand Miles in Wharfedale', 1892,
Goodall & Suddick.

W. Andrews, 'Bygone Yorkshire', 1892, A Brown & Sons.

A.H. Norway, 'Highways and Byways in Yorkshire', 1899,
Macmillan General Books.

G. Home, 'Yorkshire', 1908, A & C Black Ltd.

J. Crowther, 'Rambles Round Grassington', 1920,
T A J Waddington.

E. Bogg, 'By the Banks of the Wharfe', 1921,
J Miles (Rhodes & Sons Ltd, Printers).

E. Bogg, 'The Middle Valley of the Wharfe', 1922,
J Miles (Rhodes & Sons Ltd, Printers).

E. Bogg, 'Beautiful Wensleydale
and By the Banks of the Yore', 1925,
J Miles, (Rhodes & Sons Ltd, Printers).

H. Sutcliffe, 'The Striding Dales', 1929,
F Warne & Co Ltd.

E. Pontefract & M. Hartley, 'Swaledale', 1934,
Smith Settle.

E. Pontefract & M. Hartley, 'Wensleydale', 1936,
Smith Settle.

W. T. Palmer, 'Odd Corners in the Yorkshire Dales', 1937, Skeffington & Sons Ltd.

E. Pontefract & M. Hartley, 'Wharfedale', 1938, Smith Settle.

E. Pontefract & M. Hartley, 'Yorkshire Tour', 1939, J M Dent & Sons Ltd.

A. Mee, 'Yorkshire North Riding', 1941, Hodder & Stoughton Ltd.

A. Mee, 'Yorkshire West Riding', 1941, Hodder & Stoughton Ltd.

G. B. Wood, 'Yorkshire Tribute', 1950, Methuen.

Various, 'The Dalesman', Vols 14-21 1952 - 1960, Dalesman .Publishing.

J. & R. Fairfax- Blakeborough, 'The Spirit of Yorkshire', 1954, B. T. Batsford Ltd.

M. Hartley & J. Ingliby, 'The Wonders of Yorkshire', 1959, J. M. Dent & Sons Ltd.

A. Raistrick & J. Illingworth, 'The Face of North-West Yorkshire', 1967, Dalesman Publishing.

J. Hammond, 'Complete Yorkshire', 1973, Ward Lock Ltd.

I. Dewhirst, 'Yorkshire Through the Years', 1975, B. T. Batsford Ltd.

R. A. Carter, 'Yorkshire Churches', 1976, Watmoughs.

G. Wright, 'The Yorkshire Dales', 1977,
David & Charles.

N. Wingate & L. L. Stafford, 'Grassington and Wharfedale', 1977,
Wingate & Stafford.

N. Duerden, 'Portrait of the Dales', 1978,
R. Hale Ltd.

J. Herriot, 'James Herriot's Yorkshire', 1979,
Michael Joseph.

Ordnance Survey/AA, 'Leisure Guide Yorkshire Dales, 1985,
AA/OS.

A. Wainwright, 'Wainwright on the Pennine Way', 1985,
Michael Joseph.

F. Duerden, 'Great Walks Yorkshire Dales', 1986,
Ward Lock Ltd.

A. Wainwright, 'A Pennine Journey - The Story of
a Long Walk in 1938', 1986,
Michael Joseph.(pp11,16-17,29,30-31,36,41-42,213)
Reproduced by permission of Penguin Books Ltd.

M. Harding, 'Walking the Dales', 1986, Michael Joseph.

G. White, 'Walks in Swaledale', 1986, Dalesman.

J. Hillaby, 'John Hillaby's Yorkshire', 1986, Constable.

K. Piggin, 'Swaledale & Wensleydale', 1987,
Jarrold & Sons Ltd.

Ordnance Survey, 'The Yorkshire Dales and York', 1989,
OS/Jarrold Publications.

B. Pepper, 'A Haunt of Rare Souls
- The Old Inns and Pubs of Yorkshire', 1990, Smith Settle.

R. Thompson, 'North Yorkshire Ale', 1991, CAMRA.

J. Morrison, 'The Real Wensleydale', 1991, CP Printing.

D. Gerrard, 'The Real Swaledale', 1991, CP Printing.

W. R. Mitchell, 'High Dale Country', 1991, Souvenir Press.

A. Wainwright, 'Wainwright in the Limestone Dales', 1991,
Michael Joseph.
Reproduced by permission of Penguin Books Ltd.

J. Herriot, 'Every Living Thing', 1992, Michael Joseph.

Various, 'The Dalesman', 1975, 1986, 1988, 1990, 1993, 1994,
Dalesman Publishing.

W. Andrews, 'Picturesque Yorkshire', date unknown,
Valentine & Sons Ltd.

Fletcher, 'Nooks & Corners of Yorkshire', date unknown, Nash.
C. E. Lewis, 'Wharfedale', date unknown, S P C K.

E. Bogg, 'From Eden Vale to the Plains of York',
date unknown, Goodall & Suddick.

The Inn Way...*to the Yorkshire Dales*
LOG BOOK

. . . .

"Drinking in the scenery"

✦

Visit as many of the twenty-six pubs along The Inn Way... to the Yorkshire Dales as possible and record your progress with this Log Book. Fill in your Log Book by using the 'clippers' which can be found attached to The Inn Way 'pub signs' outside every pub, or ask for the landlord's signature. Please note - it is not necessary to visit all 26 pubs to claim your free certificate.

Send your completed Log Book to the address below to receive your free 'Inn Way' certificate (please include an A4 SAE as well as your name and address; we will return this Log Book with your certificate). Photocopies of this Log Book will not be accepted.

'The Inn Way' Merchandise & Gifts
If you would like to purchase an 'Inn Way' certificate then please write to us for a copy of 'The Inn Way' books and merchandise brochure or visit our website.

We produce a range of walking guidebooks as well as a selection of quality merchandise and gift items including 'Inn Way' branded outdoor fleeces, polo shirts, performance T-shirts, beenie hats, glass beer tankards, fabric badges, postcards featuring the pen and ink drawings from the books plus much more...

INNWAY PUBLICATIONS
102 LEEDS ROAD
HARROGATE
HG2 8HB

www.innway.co.uk

LOG BOOK PAGE ONE

Day One   Date / Time of Visit / Clip or Sign

1. Black Horse Hotel, Grassington   . . . .

2. Devonshire Hotel, Grassington   . . . .

3. Foresters Arms, Grassington   . . . .

4. Tennant Arms, Kilnsey   . . . .

5. Falcon Inn, Arncliffe   . . . .

6. Queens Arms, Litton   . . . .

7. Buck Inn, Buckden   . . . .

Day Two

8. White Lion, Cray   . . . .

9. Rose and Crown, Bainbridge   . . . .

10. Victoria Arms, Worton   . . . .

11. King's Arms Hotel, Askrigg   . . . .

12. Crown Inn, Askrigg   . . . .

Day Three

13. King's Head, Gunnerside   . . . .

14. Black Bull Hotel, Reeth   . . . .

15. King's Arms, Reeth   . . . .

16. Buck Hotel, Reeth   . . . .

LOG BOOK PAGE TWO

Day Four   Date / Time of Visit / Clip or Sign

17. Bridge Hotel, Grinton   ....

18. Wheatsheaf Hotel, Carperby   ....

19. Palmer Flatt Hotel, Aysgarth   ....

20. Fox and Hounds, West Burton   ....

Day Five

21. Thwaite Arms, Horsehouse   ....

22. King's Head, Kettlewell   ....

23. Blue Bell, Kettlewell   ....

24. Racehorses Hotel, Kettlewell   ....

Day Six

25. Clarendon Hotel, Hebden   ....

26. Fountaine Inn, Linton   ....

✦

Name ....
(as it is to appear on the certificate)

Address ....

....

Date completed. ....

Don't forget the SAE

Printed by Spectrum Print Tel: 01472 340862